Marathon 490 B.C.

Athens crushes the Persian Might

Marathon 490 B.C.

Athens crushes the Persian Might

D. BELEZOS - N. GIANNOPOULOS - I. KOTOULAS - K. GRIGOROPOULOS

"The Dilemma," painting by Christos Giannopoulos.

AUTHORS
Nikos Giannopoulos - Dimitris Belezos
Kyriakos Grigoropoulos - Ioannis Kotoulas

EDITORS (ENGLISH EDITION)
Nikos Giannopoulos, *Historian*
Stelios Demiras

TRANSLATOR
Nikos Th. Tselepides

PROOF EDITOR
Charles Davis

COVER ART
Christos Giannopoulos

UNIFORM RESEARCH AND RECONSTRUCTION
Christos Giannopoulos

ADDITIONAL ILLUSTRATIONS
Romilos Fronimidis

ART DIRECTOR
Dimitra Mitsou

COVER DESIGN
Georgia Louka

MAPS
Dimitra Mitsou

First published in Greece in 2008
by Periscopio Publications

8, G. Seferi Str., 17234, Dafni, Greece.

E-mail: info@periscopio.gr
www.periscopio.gr

© 2008 Periscopio Publications

ISBN: 978-0-89747-561-7

NIKOS GIANNOPOULOS

Nikos Giannopoulos was born in 1973 in Athens. He studied history at the History and Archeology Department of the University of Ioannina. Since 2001, he has been the Directing Editor of monographs for the "Military History" magazine and Chief Editor of the "Great Battles" magazine, both of Persicopio Editions. In addition, Nikos has written a number of articles on the military history of ancient, medieval and modern Greece. Three of his monographs, titled "Theodore Kolokotronis," "Count Dracula" and "Byzantine-Bulgarian Wars," have been published by Periscopio Publications. In June 2007, he participated as a main lecturer in the first Pan-European Congress on the Battle of Marathon that was organized by the Municipality of Marathon under the auspices of the Greek Ministry of Culture.

DIMITRIS BELEZOS

Dimitris Belezos was born in Athens in 1975. He studied history at the History and Archaeology Department of the University of Athens and has an M.A. in Modern Greek History. He has written various articles related to the ancient and medieval world for the Greek magazines concerning general and military history, published by Periscopio Publications. Four of his monographs, titled "Crusades," "The Latin Domination Era in Greece," "Alcibiades," and "The Byzantine Army," have also been published by the same publishing company.

KYRIAKOS GRIGOROPOULOS

Kyriakos Grigoropoulos was born in Athens in 1979. He studied history and archeology at the Philosophy Department of the University of Athens, graduating in 2001 with a degree in Archeology. He continued his studies at the same university and, during 2003, also studied at the University of Oxford under the ERASMUS program. Kyriakos attained his post-graduate degree in Prehistoric Archeology in 2004. At present, he is working on his doctorate degree at the University of Athens under a Greek state scholarship. As a pre- and post-graduate student, Kyriakos has participated in archeological excavations and research projects in Greece and Turkey. He has also published a number of articles on archeological and historical subjects. His primary interests include the relationships of wars, societies and ideologies, not only of the Aegean prehistoric period but also of the whole of the ancient world of the Mediterranean region.

IOANNIS KOTOULAS

Ioannis Kotoulas is a historian and was born in Sydney, Australia, in 1976. He studied history and archaeology at the National University of Athens and has an M.A. in the History of Art. He is currently writing his dissertation on "Neogothic Tradition in European Architecture and in Greece" at the same university. He is the scientific editor and translator of the series "Historical Archives of World War II" (Athens, Periplous Publications, 2007). Six of his monographs, titled "Vikings," "The Peloponnesian War," "The Army of Alexander the Great," "Josef Stalin," "The Rise of the Third Reich," and "Axis War Crimes," have been published by Periscopio Publications, and "Intellectuals and Power" was published by Periplous Publications. Many of his articles have been published in various historical magazines by Periscopio Publications and in the Sunday editions of the newspaper Vima.

CHRISTOS GIANNOPOULOS

Christos Giannopoulos, an illustrator and figure designer, was born in 1968 in Athens. Although he has a degree and professional experience in Social Work, he has developed a special interest in ancient and medieval history. Christos has worked for 14 years as a professional artist and has produced illustrations for many children's titles, multimedia projects, and a number of books on ancient, medieval, and modern warfare. With his unlimited interest in figure design and uniform research, Christos has created original illustrations that have been a source of inspiration for a number of miniature sculptors producing figures for model companies, including Romeo Models and Pegaso Models of Italy, and Seil Models of Korea. His favored fields of study and research are Ancient Greek hoplite warfare, Celtic Europe, Central Asian cultures, and Roman Britain.

Contents

Preface

If one thinks of the great contribution of classical-period Athens to predominantly European but also world culture in general, then one easily understands what was at stake on that morning in 490 B.C. at Marathon, when the hoplites of Athens with their Plataean allies repulsed the might of the Persian Empire. The Athenians, in addition to their political independence, also defended the right of the human spirit to think freely. If the city had been destroyed, we would never have been privy to the Golden Age of Pericles, and the thinkers of Athens would never have spread their philosophical enlightenment, literature or other contributions to the far corners of the world.

Contemporary historians claim that the Battle of Marathon was not of decisive importance, as the Persians did return 10 years later. However, they have not considered the possibility that, even if the Persians had stopped with the destruction and subjugation of the city, there was no force able to prevent them from later launching a new campaign that would have led to the conquest of the whole of Greece. Sparta was the only other significant power of the period, but it is doubtful if Sparta alone would have been capable of stopping a Persian invasion.

The glory achieved by the Marathon warriors at the battle cannot be compared with any other human accomplishment. For the great tragic poet Aeschylus, who saw a Persian ax remove life from his own brother, Cynaigeiros, that day was monumental. The creator of "Oresteia" and "Prometheus Bound" requested, a short time before his death, that the following epigram be inscribed on his tombstone: "This tomb covers Aeschylus, the Athenian, son of Euphorion. For his renowned valor can speak the sacred Marathonian grove and the Persian with the long hair, who knew it well." He says nothing about his poetry, and nothing about his participation in the naval battles of Artemisium and Salamis. The only things mentioned are the "Marathonian grove" and his "renowned valor" on the day when he fought in the phalanx and defended the freedom of his city as a mere hoplite.

With the passing of time, the aura of a fascinating legend has covered the battlefield of Marathon and "each night one can still feel the neighing of horses and the sounds of the battle of men."

Nikos Giannopoulos
Editor

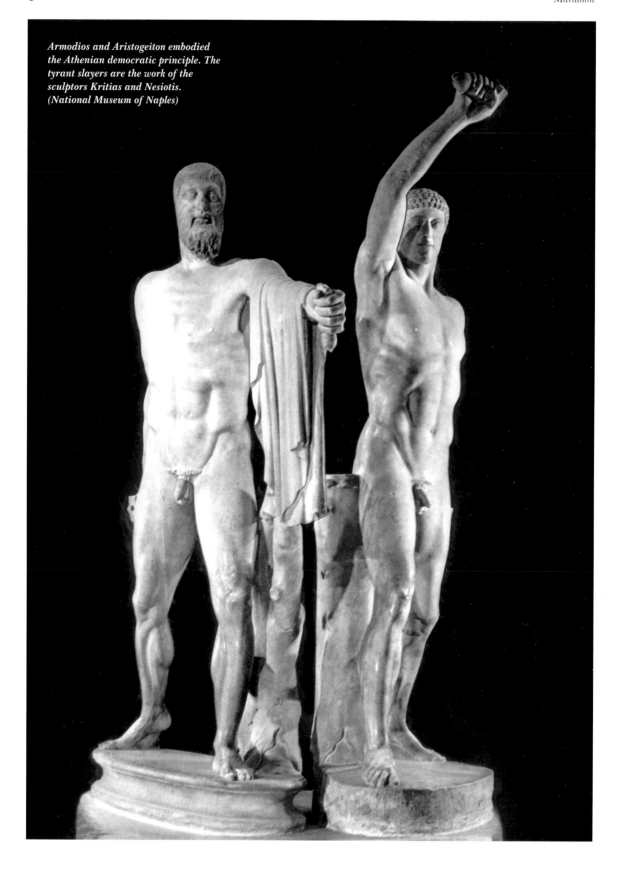

Armodios and Aristogeiton embodied the Athenian democratic principle. The tyrant slayers are the work of the sculptors Kritias and Nesiotis. (National Museum of Naples)

Political and military organization of Athens

The character of the city that deflated Persian arrogance

Athens, at the time of the Marathon battle still existed in the aftermath of major political changes that had influenced the military and social structures, and had laid the foundations for the future Athenian dominance in Greece. In the second half of the sixth century B.C., the tyrant Peisistratus dominated the life of Athens. After his death in 528 B.C., his sons, Hippias and Hipparchus, succeeded him. During the first years of their rule, the system of tyrannical government was transformed. Whereas Peisistratus had lived like a simple citizen and always tried to avoid offending the sensibilities of the Athenians by improper behavior, his sons surrounded themselves with a coterie of people consisting mainly of poets and artists. This fact did not, of course, create a negative impression as this clique of the intelligentsia, the Peisistratids, contributed to the fame of Athens as a center of Greek civilization. At that time, the members of the old aristocratic Athenian families that had been exiled from the city during the rule of Peisistratus were now allowed to return. These aristocrats now felt secure in Athens and, with the tyrants' consent, some among them even ran for public office, but never gained significant political power.

The Battle of Marathon is one of the foremost achievements in the history of Athens. The major contributing factor to victory was the political system of Athens. Cleisthenis had created this less than two decades before the 490 B.C. Persian invasion. The political developments associated with the emergence of the new form of government must be described in some detail, not merely because they help to understand the military organization of Athens at that time, but also because the new political system contributed to the greatest achievement of ancient Greece, namely the establishment of free people such as the Marathon hoplites.

The demise of the Peisistratids

Despite the unease among the aristocratic families, no major effort was undertaken to oust the tyrants during the first years of Peisistatus' sons' rule. The start of the effort to remove tyranny is contributed to a seemingly insignificant event of a personal nature. According to contemporary sources, Hippias made sexual advances toward Harmodius, a handsome youth, and was rejected. To take his revenge, Hippias insulted Harmodius' sister. Harmodius asked his friend, Aristogeiton, to help him punish the tyrant. The two friends, in cooperation with other Athenians, attempted the assassination of Hippias during the Panathenaic Festival. On the chosen day, they were surprised to discover that a strong bodyguard was with the tyrant. The conspirators quickly realized that their plan had been discovere and, consequently, they would soon be arrested. However, as they were determined to act before being arrested, they attacked and killed the unsuspecting Hipparchus. Following the assassination of his brother, Hippias changed the moderate, more forgiving ways he had adopted until then. He became harder and forced the aristocrats who had returned to Athens to abandon it once again.

The most interesting aspect of the effort to weaken the powers of the Peisistratids and to establish the Athenian political system following the fall of tyranny was the neutral and somewhat indifferent reaction exhibited by the Athenian population. It is worth noting that most of the lower-class Athenians were followers of Peisistratus. While they may have felt disturbed by the rule of Peisistratus' sons, it is doubtful they desired the return of the old aristocratic system of government. On the other hand, the aristocratic families sought the help of the king of Sparta, Cleomenes, and asked him for his support in order to return to Athens. Finally, in 510 B.C., due to the intervention of the Spartan army, Hippias was forced to quit Athens, four years after Hipparchus' assassination. The ousting of the tyrant was a triumph for the Athenian

aristocracy, although they were unable to cling to power for long. It was these developments that laid the foundations for the future Persian invasion at Marathon.

Hippias, meanwhile, took refuge in Persia, where he acted as a counselor for matters related to Greece. In parallel, the Persians had found in him a person who could be used to both destabilize and influence events in Attica and the central Aegean region in general, according to the plans and decisions of the Persian ruler at any given moment.

After the fall of tyranny, two leading Athenian citizens clashed over matters relating to the city's future. One was Teisandrus' son, Isagoras, a representative of the older aristocracy, while the other was Cleisthenes, a member of the influential Alcmeonids family. Cleisthenes' family was connected politically with the residents of the city, i.e., the inhabitants of central Athens. Many of the city's residents were merchants and artisans who had acquired large estates. They wanted more civil rights as they already enjoyed a fair amount of financial power. However, the aristocrats reacted strongly against this idea as they saw their powers threatened by the "nouveau riche." However, Cleisthenes had many followers and lived near the city center where the Athenian state's central power also had its seat. This caused uneasiness among Isagoras and his followers and they once again called upon King Cleomenes for assistance. It is said that the Spartan king arrived before the city with his army and had even occupied the Acropolis itself. The Athenians reacted strongly against this outrage, and Cleomenes was forced to depart in the face of such opposition. It is possible that, subsequently, the Spartan king was unable to find a way to explain to his subjects why he intervened in the internal affairs of Athens and that he feared facing the accusation of conducting policies born of self-interest. Thus, in 508 B.C., Cleisthenes and his followers gained control of the city with enough power to influence its politics according to their interests and principles.

The 10 tribes and their military role

Initially, Cleisthenes retained the division of Athenians into categories in accordance with their income, as Solon had prescribed. The highest class was the Pentakosiomedimnoi, with a minimum annual income of 500 medimnoi of grain. The medimnos were the measuring unit of agricultural produce. The next class was the Hippeis, or the Triakosiomedimnoi. These two premier classes, the Pentakosiomedimnoi and the Triakosiomedimnoi, enjoyed more civil rights due to their greater wealth. However, the main body of Athenian society was the third class, known as Zeugitai or Diakosiomedimnoi. This class consisted of small farmers who, in time of war, served as foot infantry in the hoplite phalanx. In contrast, the two higher classes of the Pentakosiomedimnoi and the Triakosiomedimnoi fought as cavalry. Finally, the lowest class was the Thetes, the non-land-owning inhabitants seeking a redistribution of land in order to improve their income. In time of war, these people fought as lightly armed infantry (psiloi), although they did not receive great respect from their fellow citizens as they did not contribute to the defense of Athens to any significant degree and were also viewed as a source of possible social unrest. Later,

when Athens developed into a major naval power, the Thetes were afforded more rights as they began to serve as rowers in the Athenian triremes. Meanwhile, while Athens depended heavily on its cavalry and hoplites, the Thetes were of marginal significance.

The most significant Cleisthenian reforms were the abolition of the older political, social, and military structures of Athens. Until then, Athenian citizenry had been divided into four tribes. These divisions had been established according to the old Ionian tradition. Each tribe had been subdivided into "gene" (clans) from which the basic military unit was

An illustration depicting an ancient Corinthian Greek helmet.

formed. Through these clans, the old aristocratic families had formed clientele relationships among a great part of the population. In order to abolish this state of affairs, Cleisthenes replaced the four old tribes with ten new ones. Attica was divided into three regions – the coast, the city, and the plain. Each of these regions was subdivided into 10 trittyes (groups), each of which consisted of unions of neighboring settlements. The 30 trittyes were further unified into groups of three to form 10 tribes. Each tribe had to have one trittys (group) from each Athenian region – i.e., one from the coast, one from the city, and one from the plain.

The 10 new tribes thus formed were given names of Athenian heroes, which were approved by the Delphic Oracle. The members of each tribe elected their representatives among the common administrative and executive organs of the Athenian state and fought together in time of war. To facilitate conscription, it was determined that the demarchos (mayor or chief official) of each demes, i.e., each sizeable municipality, would be responsible for maintaining the list of citizens in his municipality. This list included all the names of the free citizens over 18 years of age. Those able to render military service had to man the ranks of their tribe's military force. Each tribe was required to supply a hoplite regiment and a squadron of cavalry who were commanded by a general (strategos) from each tribe. For practical, political, and military reasons, it was necessary to stabilize the number of citizens of each deme. It was further determined that all Athenians were to retain their registration in the same deme and, therefore, in the same tribe in which their forebears had registered during the Cleisthenian reforms. In this way,

the Athenian army was able to stabilize the number of foot soldiers and cavalrymen each tribe contributed.

The 10 generals (strategoi) were initially under the command of the Archon Polemarch (Chief Warlord), who held one of the oldest Athenian offices that had survived the Cleisthenian reforms. The Archon Polemarch was part of the group of 10 archons (leaders). The remainder of the army commanders consisted of three additional Archons, these three office holders being known as the Archon Eponymos (Designated Leader), the Polemarch, and the Archon Basileus (King Leader), and six Thesmothetai who acted as judges and interpreters of law. The citizens belonging to the higher classes of the Pentakosiomedimnoi and the Triakosiomedimnoi elected the nine Archons and the Archon Polemarch. This made the military higher command of Athens appear oligarchic in nature. Gradually, however, the power of the Archon Polemarch diminished as the power of the generals rose proportionately. A common element between the Archon Polemarch and the generals was that their term of office was limited to one year. Gifted politicians often managed to get re-elected as generals and to pursue a successful career in politics through re-election.

The Council of the 500 and the Public Assembly (Ecclesia of the Deme)

The two most important governmental organs in Cleisthenes' Athenian polity were the Public Assembly (Ecclesia of the Deme) and the Council (Vouli) of the 500. The Council of the 500 was elected for a term of one year. Each of the 10 tribes was represented by 50 council members. Each deme of a tribe was represented by a pre-determined number of members. The council members (vouleutai) were drawn by lot. The duty of the council was to check the administrative work and behavior of the Archons and to supervise economic management. The council was also responsible for matters related to foreign policy, security and defense, though it had no power to declare war or make peace. Decisions on such important matters as the latter were the exclusive responsibility of the Public Assembly. However, no matter could be discussed in the assembly if it had not first been approved and introduced for debate by the Council of the 500.

For more efficient functioning of the council, especially in urgent matters relating to administrative practices and internal and external security, the annual tenure of the council was subdivided into 10 periods. Within each of these periods, the Council members of one specific tribe held greater authority and were thus designated prytaneis (presidents), while their tribe was named the prytanevousa tribe (presiding tribe). Each day, and for just one 24-hour period, one member of the 50 presidents was selected by lot to serve as the foreman (epistates). He was obliged to stay for one day in the prytaneum – the public building that had been built to house the prytaneis in the agora of Athens. The council members of one prytanevousa trittys (presiding tribal group) stayed with the foreman. If an emergency occurred, they were on duty and ready to confront the situation. The Athenian state provided them with free food to facilitate them in their duties.

The highest ruling body in the Athenian state was essentially the Public Assembly, consisting of all free Athenian citizens. This, of course, was a mere formality as the members of the lower classes, in Cleisthenes' time and, later still, at the time of the Battle of Marathon, held no privilege to participate in public assemblies. In addition, many of the thetes lived far from the city where the Public Assembly met and travel into Athens was tiring. No economic reward had yet been instituted for those citizens who participated in the Public Assembly meetings, which meant that if the poor people wished to participate, they would have to leave their work and lose valuable income. The Athenian polity during the period of the Persian invasion had not yet reached its final form, which was to flourish later as the democracy of the Plato era. Indeed, even though there was a principled foundation capable of leading to further democratic development, the government of the state was still exercised by the higher classes of the pentakosiomedimnoi and the triakosiomedimnoi, who had the economic power to devote time to politics. It was, however, due to the reforms of Cleisthenes that the power of the diakosiomedimnoi middle class was strengthened, and these were the hoplites who saved Athens at the battle on the Marathon plain.

The Ionian Revolt
The great first clash between Greeks and Persians

The efforts by the Greek cities of the Eastern Aegean to break free of Persian rule resulted in a fierce clash on both land and sea in which the Persian and Greek military forces were tested hard for the first time. The Persian final victory was due primarily to organizational problems and lack of cooperation among the Greeks, leading the Persian king, Darius, to falsely assess his prospects of victory in a future invasion of Greece.

During the sixth century B.C., the Greek city-states in Asia Minor represented the center of Greek civilization. The cities were divided into three groups. Along the northernmost region of the eastern Aegean coast were the Aeolian settlements. Along the central part of the eastern coast were the cities of the Ionians and the Ionian islands of Chios and Samos across the sea. It was within these Ionian settlements that the greatest amount of cultural activity and wealth of the Greeks was concentrated. Further south, on the islands of Cos and Rhodes and on the adjacent coast, lay the cities founded by the Dorians. The cities of mainland Greece could not be compared to those of Asia Minor, as even the cities of wealthy Corinth, powerful Sparta, and famed Athens appeared insignificant when compared with Miletus, Ephesus, and other smaller cities of Asia Minor. The Ionian Greeks had developed commercial

trade with many areas of the Mediterranean and had founded more colonies than all the Greeks of mainland Greece. Miletus alone was the central metropolis for numerous colonies. Commerce brought about a great cultural flourish allied to economic wealth to the cities of the Ionian coast. The Ionian cities possessed impressive temples that were distinguished for the quality of their architecture, decorative elements, and size. The sages of Ionia had already begun to study nature and to lay the foundations of modern science and philosophy.

The Greek cities of Asia Minor, despite the advantages offered by their geographical location, also had a significant disadvantage because they lay unprotected from the powerful barbarian kingdoms to the east. The first barbarian ruler who imposed his rule on the Asia Minor Greeks was Croesus, the king of Lydia. His kingdom encompassed the central and western region of Asia Minor and his capital, Sardis, was one of the richest cities in the region and ranked with the finest cities on the coast in influence. Croesus became king of Lydia in 560 B.C. and one of his first acts was to besiege Ephesus and force its tyrant, Pindar, to flee the city. After he had established his dominance over Ephesus, Croesus forced the Greek cities to pay an annual subjugation tax and to contribute men to his armed forces whenever he required them. The city of Miletus, the Aeolian, and, probably, the Dorian cities escaped the Lydian subjugation. Despite this

The ruins of Ephesus. This city and Eretria played a leading role in the Ionian Revolt.

situation, Croesus' rule was not unduly oppressive as he always allowed the Greeks to run their internal affairs as they wished and to select their own form of government. Under these conditions, Ephesus was able to establish a democratic government that lasted until its conquest by the Persians. Furthermore, Croesus was an admirer of Greek civilization and had financed the construction of the temple of Artemis in Ephesus. Because of his financial support, this temple became so grandiose that it was designated as one of the Seven Wonders of the Ancient World. Croesus also showed equal respect for the Greek oracles and often offered rich gifts to the sacred Oracle of Delphi. It is also probable that Croesus contributed in the development of commerce between the Ionians and the Egyptians, as he was an ally of the Pharaoh Amasi. Egypt was a key area for Ionian exports, and the Ionians had even founded a colony on the Nile delta, the city of Naucratis.

The Persian Conquest

In 550 B.C., a mere 10 years after Croesus attained the throne, the Lydian kingdom was threatened on its eastern flank. Cyrus II, the Persian king, defeated the Medes and united the kingdoms of Persia and Media into a powerful new state. This worried Croesus, and he decided to attack the new kingdom. He first sought and obtained the approval of the Greek oracles, whose opinions he respected and honored, and then sought an alliance with Sparta, knowing that the Spartans were excellent warriors. Sparta obliged and declared itself an ally but did not have sufficient time to take part in the battle in which the Lydians were ultimately defeated. In 546 B.C., Cyrus occupied Sardis and conquered the Lydian kingdom. Throughout the war, the Persian king had urged the Greeks of Asia Minor to revolt against Croesus and so facilitate his invasion, but the Greeks had refused, believing that the Lydian kingdom was strong enough to resist and would eventually win the war. In addition, the Greeks felt that Lydian dominance was not at all oppressive and it assured them of commercial expansion and rich gifts for the Greek temples from the generous Lydian monarch.

Following the conquest of Lydia, the Asia Minor Greeks sent delegates to Cyrus with the offer of remaining his subjects on the same conditions as those specified by Croesus. Cyrus, however, reminded them of the recalcitrance of the Greek cities to support him in the war against the Lydians, making it clear that he had no intention of changing the prevailing conditions. He was, however, willing to make one exception for the Miletians, as they were not part of the kingdom of Lydia. Worried by this development, the inhabitants of the Greek cities decided to organize their defense. Their representatives gathered in the Panionium, the religious sanctuary of worship of the Asia Minor Ionians, and decided to ask the Spartans for assistance. While the Aeolian cities allied themselves with the Greeks in order to face the common enemy, the island city-states did not enter the alliance as they felt that the Persians would not threaten them, as they possessed no navy of any importance. One of the first acts of the Ionians and Aeolians was to send envoys to Sparta. The most important envoy among them was Pythermus from Phocia who had been tasked with speaking to the Spartans on behalf of all the cities of Asia Minor. The Spartans, for their part, avoided making any concrete promises but did send a delegation to Asia Minor to study the situation in the region while sending word to Cyrus that they would not tolerate a Persian attack against any Greek city. Cyrus did not appear particularly impressed by this warning, but problems emerging in other regions of the Persian Empire forced him to cancel his expedition into Asia Minor.

The Persian Dominance in Ionia

While Cyrus was away, a Lydian official, Pactyas, prepared the revolt by his compatriots against the Persians. This revolt soon spread across the whole of Lydia as the only Persian garrison was at Sardis. Pactyas was soon able to gain the trust of the Greeks who supported him in the belief that a resurrection of the Lydian

A map of the Greek cities of the eastern coast of Asia Minor.

kingdom would lift the Persian threat. When Cyrus was informed of the Lydian revolt, he immediately dispatched Mazares to Asia Minor with orders to crush Pactyas' army, which he accomplished very quickly. Once this was done, Mazares turned against the remaining Greek cities. He conquered the Ionian Greek city-states of Priene and Magnesia on the Maeander looting and plundering as he went, but he died before he had time to advance farther afield. Harpagus, who went on to besiege Phocia, succeeded Mazares. The Phocians sought to purchase the island of Oinoussai from the people of Chios in order to relocate their city there, but without success. Half of the city's population of Phocia decided to migrate to Alalia, a colony they had founded on Corsica, while the remainder opted to stay in Asia Minor and suffer Persian domination. In many ways, the fate of the rest of the Asia Minor Greek city-states was similar. While many tried to resist, they lacked organization and the necessary coordination due to poor communication. The Persians were thus able to conquer all the coastal area Greek cities in a few years. Those people not willing to live under Persian rule fled to the colonies of the western Mediterranean. Bias of Priene, one of the Seven Sages of Ancient Greece, went so far as to declare that all the Greeks of the Asia Minor coast should migrate to Sardenia and establish new cities there, which would be safe from the Persian threat, as he felt the Greeks would be unable to successfully face this threat. He also stated that even if the Greek cities managed to ward off all the Persian assaults, they would

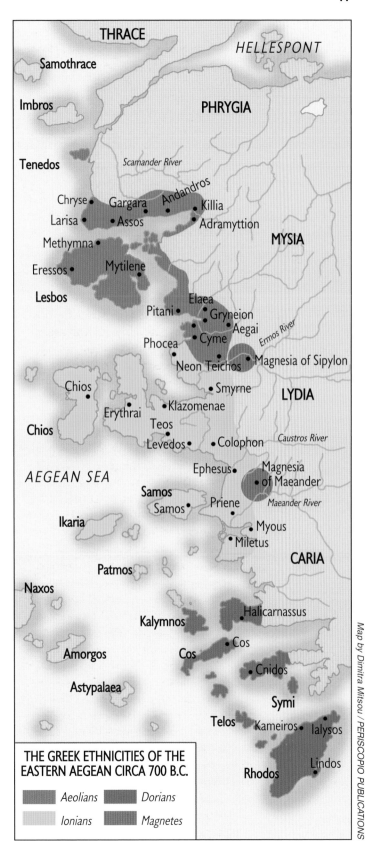

THE GREEK ETHNICITIES OF THE EASTERN AEGEAN CIRCA 700 B.C.

Aeolians   Dorians

Ionians   Magnetes

Map by Dimitra Mitsou / PERISCOPIO PUBLICATIONS

always remain exposed to further attacks in the future. The Asia Minor Greeks, however, rejected his arguments and came under Persian rule. Shortly after, the cities of the nearby islands of the eastern Aegean followed suit. The last cities to submit to Persian rule were the Dorian cities of the eastern Aegean. The Greek cities under Persian domination were obliged to pay a subjugation tax to the Persian king and to provide men for his army. It should be noted that the Dorian cities were conquered with help of army contingents contributed by the subjugated Ionians and Aeolians of Asia Minor.

The Persians imposed their own trusted tyrants in the Asia Minor coastal areas in order to safeguard their conquests. The Persian satrap residing in Sardis who was directly under the orders of the Persian king supervised the actions of these tyrants. All meetings of the various assemblies of the free citizenry were banned, and commercial exchanges with other areas of the Mediterranean were curtailed. The decrease in the commercial activities of the Asia Minor Greeks was due to the fact that their most important commercial competitors, namely the Phoenicians on the Libyan coast, were now under Persian rule. The Persian kingdom had no particular reason to support the Asia Minor Greeks' commercial initiatives in the way the Lydian kingdom had supported them in the past. Furthermore, the conquest of Egypt by the Persians in 545 B.C. had further restricted the commercial exchanges between the Ionians and the countries of the Nile delta. The city of Sybaris in Lower Italy, a commercial partner of Miletus, was destroyed by the Crotonians in 510 B.C., this financial disaster being so severe for the Miletians that they declared a period of national mourning. The Persian kingdom could not, of course, be held responsible for the destruction of the Greek city in Italy, but the ensuing economic crisis created even greater dislike of Persian rule.

The tyrant Histiaeus

In the late sixth century B.C., the tyrant Histiaeus, an extremely ambitious and treacherous man who had accompanied the Persian king during his campaign against the Scythians who inhabited the north side of the Danube River, ruled the city of Miletus.

In 513 B.C., Darius crossed into Europe with a great army and headed north, with the intention of conquering the Scythian barbarians. The Persian army reached the Danube, built bridges, and crossed to its northern bank. Darius entrusted the guarding of these bridges to the tyrants of the Greek cities of Asia Minor and the Greek hoplites under their command. Meanwhile, the Scythians involved the Persians in a constant war of attrition by a series of surprise attacks. The Scythian leaders then proposed to the Greek tyrants that they destroy the bridges so they could trap the Persians on the northern side of the Danube where they could be annihilated. The majority of the tyrants viewed this plan as a very good opportunity to free themselves of Persian domination. Miltiades the Athenian, the general of the city of Athens' army in the later Battle of Marathon, advised the tyrants to comply with the Scythian request. At that time, Miltiades was governor of a small hegemony created by an uncle who bore the same name and was himself a subject of the Persians and was, at that particular moment, taking part in the campaign against the Scythians.

Histiaeus, who was quite influential as he was the ruling tyrant of one of the most important and wealthiest Greek cities, disagreed with Miltiades' proposal. He reminded the rest of the tyrants that they had been appointed to their offices by the Persians, stressing the fact that, if the Persian force were defeated, nothing stood in the way of the inhabitants of the cities of Asia Minor who waited for a chance to eliminate all the hated ruling tyrants. His arguments being very persuasive, the tyrants agreed not to destroy the bridges. This decision saved the Persian army and King Darius from total annihilation. To show his gratitude, the Persian king rewarded Histiaeus by giving him the settlement at Myrcinus on the river Strymon, an area of rich silver mines and vast timber forests.

When Histiaeus took over the Myrcinus area, he fortified its defenses. However, this development worried the satrap of Sardis, Megabazus, who proceeded to inform Darius what the tyrant of Miletus was doing, adding that these measures were calculated to bring about the creation of an economic and military base in the northern Aegean. Darius perceived the dangers involved and ordered Histiaeus to Susa to advise the Persians on matters related to Ionia. On his arrival at Sardis, Histiaeus, to his surprise, discovered he could not return to Miletus. On top of that, a new city tyrant, his son-in-law Aristagoras, had already replaced him. Despite this, he was not arrested at Sardis but remained free and the Persians used him as an advisor, although taking care not to allow him to return to Miletus. The Ionian Revolt may have been Histiaeus' original idea in the belief that through it he could leave Sardis and return to Miletus. In other words, he believed that if the Greeks of Asia Minor revolted, Darius would be forced to send him back to Miletus to suppress the revolt. Such a premise was plausible, as Histiaeus knew Ionia well and was in secret communication with Aristagoras.

The start of the Ionian Revolt

Apart from Histiaeus' schemes and conspiracies, the spark that precipitated the revolt of the Greek cities of Asia Minor was the failure of the Persian siege of the island of Naxos. The democrats had overthrown the oligarchy on this island, forcing the oligarchy to seek refuge in Artistagoras' court and to request his help in regaining their power. Aristagoras viewed their situation as an excellent opportunity to gain control of the eastern Aegean and strengthen his power. At the beginning, considering the size and wealth of Naxos, Aristagoras hesitated, but he finally decided that such an operation could be successful and asked Artaphernes, the satrap of Sardis, for assistance. He persuaded him that the operation would be easy and would lead to Persian dominance of the Aegean Sea. Artaphernes complied and ordered the assembly of a fleet of 200 vessels, coming mainly from the Greek cities of Asia Minor. Aristagoras was given command of the fleet, with the Persian Megabates as second-in-command. However, the operation did not go according to plan. The Naxians had been forewarned of the approaching danger and had time to organize

An Athenian hoplite. His excellent physical condition, great strength, intensive training, and superior weapons made him the most dreaded opponent for any army of antiquity. (Athens, National Archeological Museum)

their defenses. It is not clear who forewarned them, but the ancient historian Herodotus states that it was no other than Megabates himself, who had fallen into disagreement with Aristagoras and had no real wish for the expedition to succeed. It is also quite probable that the information reached the Naxians via the ships' crews of Aristagoras' fleet. It has also been claimed that Aristagoras' plan was not really to conquer Naxos, but to use the campaign as an opportunity to gather the forces of the Asia Minor Greeks and have them ready for the revolt he had planned with Histiaeus without arousing Persian suspicions. If this claim is true, it is possible that Histiaeus may have forewarned the Naxians of the approaching siege of their island. The only certain fact is that Aristagoras' fleet arrived at Naxos in the summer of 499 B.C. and laid siege to the town for four months without success. Aristagoras feared

that the Persians would hold him accountable for drawing them into this misadventure, and it was possible that they would ask him to pay the expenses incurred or would relieve him of his post as tyrant. For these reasons, and after consulting with Histiaeus, he decided the time had come for the Ionian Revolt to start.

In 499 B.C., Aristagoras held a meeting of the Ionians in Melitus at which he incited them to actively participate in a revolt against Persian rule. Simultaneously, he replaced the tyrannical form of rule of the city with a democratic one. His actions brought him the support of his fellow citizens, along with the inhabitants of the cities of the Asia Minor coast and of the adjacent islands. Only Hecataeus of Miletus, one of the most famous philosophers of the period, attempted to dissuade the Greeks from such a bold, dangerous undertaking. With the aid of a large map of the world that he had drawn up, he showed them the size of the area occupied by his fellow citizens in comparison with the immense size of the Persian kingdom that was also clearly shown.

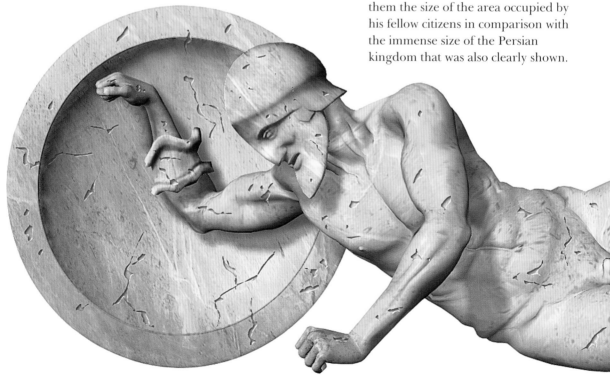

Despite this, the Miletians could not be dissuaded. Hecataeus then urged them to utilize the treasures of the Temple of Apollo at Didyma, one of the largest Greek sanctuaries, to pay for the construction of a fleet. Hecataeus argued that, if the revolt proved successful, the Miletians would be able to donate much more treasure to Apollo than that which they were about to take from him in this period of crisis. On the other hand, if the revolt failed, the Temple treasures would also be lost, as the Persians would plunder them. Despite these forceful arguments, Hecataeus' advice was not heeded.

The Ionians seek military aid

In its initial phase, the Ionian Revolt succeeded without much difficulty. The Asia Minor Greeks took control of the fleet anchored at Myus and drove the tyrants from their cities. Everywhere there was a feeling of euphoria. However, those who were aware of the actual situation and the power of the Persians waited in trepidation for Darius' reaction to the Ionian challenge. As the Asia Minor Greeks waited to see what the Persians would do, they used the time to try to gain support from the other side of the Aegean, in particular from Sparta and Athens. The Athenians belonged to the Ionian race and had even claimed that Attica was the starting point from which the Ionians had spread toward the eastern regions of the Aegean. Athens also had a sizeable population and could contribute both armed forces and money to aid the Ionians. Sparta, for its part, was the strongest military power in Greece and had made known its intention to help the Ionians in the past when it had warned Cyrus against threatening the Asia Minor Greek cities.

Aristagoras, who initially tried to gain the confidence of the Spartan king Cleomenes, the elder brother of the renowned hero Leonidas, headed the Ionian delegation sent to Athens and Sparta. Aristagoras attended the first meeting carrying a map, an Ionian invention unknown to the Spartans at that time, and attempted to analyze all the Persian kingdom's weaknesses while showing the menace it constituted for the Greek world. He also explained to Cleomenes the Persians' weapons and tactics and tried to persuade him that the Greeks were superior in these matters if they were able to muster sufficient military forces to face the massed armies that the Persian king was likely to throw into battle. Cleomenes, however, feared that sending a large number of Spartans away from the Peloponnesus might encourage the helots and the

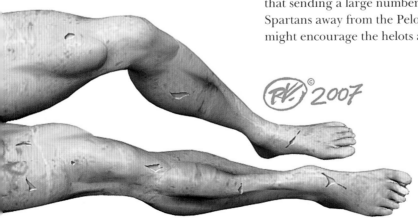

This illustration is based on a sculpture of a dying Greek hoplite from the pediment of the Temple of Aphaia on the island of Aegina. The shield and helmet are faithfully reproduced but the cuirass is absent, possibly to show the magnificent body of the heroic warrior. (illustration by Romilos Fronimidis)

perioikoi to revolt. Aristagoras then tried to tempt the Spartan king with the promise that he would become the king of Persia. In Aristagoras' opinion, the Lacedaemonian's great military expertise could be better used in a plan of grander scale rather than wasting it on small, local conflicts with its neighbors in the Peloponnesus.

At the next meeting between the two men, the Lacedaemonian king asked how far it was between the Persian capital and the Aegean coast. Aristagoras answered frankly, saying that a journey of three months was needed to get from Miletus to the heart of Persia. Herodotus states that when Cleomenes heard this, he immediately ordered Aristagoras to leave his city as he thought that the Spartans would never acquiesce to participate in such a far-flung campaign. According the Herodotus, Aristagoras then visited Cleomenes at his home to plead with him further, even to the extent of attempting to bribe him, first offering 10 talents, later increasing it to 50 talents of gold. However, Gorgo, the king's young daughter who was just 9 years old at the time, intervened, warning her further that this strange foreigner could corrupt him. Following his daughter's intervention, Cleomenes ceased all further discussion, and Aristagoras was forced to leave Sparta empty-handed. However, to a Spartan historian, this tale appears to be an exaggeration, as under no circumstances could Cleomones alone decide for or against Spartan participation in such a fraught campaign. Even if he had backed Aristagoras' proposal with all his royal authority, it is still uncertain whether he would have convinced the viceroy of Sparta, Demaratus, and the Assembly of the Spartans. Whatever may, or may not have taken place, the final result was that Aristagoras was unsuccessful in obtaining Spartan assistance.

His meeting with the Athenians, however, met with better success. The Public Assembly of Athens accepted a proposal to send 20 triremes to Ionia with Melanthius as their commander, although this force was very small when seen in the light of Attica's large population and land area. What is more, the Athenians had special reasons to want to halt Persian aggression as, it will be remembered, Hippias, Athens' former tyrant and son of Peisistratus, had taken refuge in the Persian court when he had been deposed in 511 B.C. Since then, he had been trying to return to power in Athens with Persian support. In addition, five further ships, a contribution by the city of Eretria, were added to those of Athens as a grateful gesture for the help the Miletians had given the Eretrians in their war against the people of Chalkis. The fleet's 25 ships were assembled on the Aegean's western coast and were able to transport 2,000 hoplites. However, although these forces were insignificant when compared to the might of the Persians, the military aid donated by Athens and Eretria arrived by sea in Asia Minor in 498 B.C.

The destruction of Sardis and the Persians' initial reaction

Despite the expected Persian attack, the Asia Minor Greeks were unable to organize their defenses or make any joint plans. All they did was mint a new common piece of coinage, so the main burden of military preparations remained with the city of

The ruins of the city of Salamis in Cyprus, the Greek population of which was the first to revolt against the Persians.

Miletus. Contrary to earlier Greek hopes, the revolt did not spread to Lydia, a land that could be used to halt the Persian advance while also supplying urgently needed allied forces for the coastal cities. Nonetheless, in the revolt's first clash, the Greek fleet managed to destroy the Phoenician fleet off the coast of Pamphylia. Meanwhile, Aristagoras allowed the Paeonians, who had lived on the banks of the river Strymon and who had been forced by the Persians to move into the interior of Phrygia, to return to their homeland. When the Ionian Revolt broke out, the Paeonians had secretly left Phrygia, taking their families, and had headed for the Ionian coast. From there, with the help of the Greeks, they had crossed over to Chios Island and eventually reached their homeland. Despite this success, the operation offered no substantial protection to the Greek cities. On the contrary, it focused the Persians on the fact that the Ionian Revolt had to be suppressed quickly if the Greeks were not to create further problems in Asia Minor. While the Greek cities on the coast remained unpunished, it was possible that the Lydians would follow their example and this could lead to the whole of Asia Minor freeing itself of Persian rule.

Perhaps the most daring operation of the Ionian Revolt was due to the Greeks' desire to draw the Lydians to revolt as well. Aristagoras' brother, Charopinos, undertook to lead an Ionian force, which also included the Athenian hoplites, in an attack on Sardis, the old Lydian capital and seat of the Persian satrap of Asia Minor. This combined force managed to capture the city, but the Persian garrison led by the satrap, Artaphernes, took refuge on its acropolis. While the Greeks laid siege to the Sardis acropolis, a fire broke out in the lower area of the city, and quickly spread. As the houses were mostly built of bamboo, the conflagration consumed most of the city. Following the destruction of Sardis, the Greeks were forced to retreat to the coast because the Persian army was approaching from the east.

Charopinos prudently recalled his forces and joined them with the rest of the Miletian army so they presented a united face to the enemy. The Greek and Persian armies met in battle near Ephesus in the summer of 498 B.C., with the Greeks being defeated and Eualcides, the Eretrian general, being slain in the battle. After this failure, the Athenians and Eretrians decided to return to their home cities, although Aristagoras tried, unsuccessfully, to dissuade them. The Persians, for their part, were not to forget the Athenian participation in the destruction of Sardis. According to Herodotus, when Xerxes was informed that the Athenians had assisted the Ionians in their revolt, he launched an arrow into the sky and asked the gods to allow him to punish them. He also ordered a slave to remind him of the Athenian perfidy three times a day at meal times.

Despite the departure of the Athenians and Eretrians, the Greeks of Asia Minor did not lose heart. Judging that the Persians held the advantage in land warfare, they decided not to risk any further battles or operations in the interior of Asia Minor but to take advantage of their superiority at sea. Initially, the Greek fleet sailed to the Hellespont, where it persuaded all the Greek cities in the area to join the revolt. By doing this, the Ionians placed the Euxinus passage under their control and also took an important step toward maintaining and expanding their commerce. These successes, and the additional fame gained by their conquest of Sardis, persuaded more areas to join the Ionian Revolt. Caria, with its populations already influenced by Greek civilization, followed the example of the Ionians. The Greeks of Cyprus, with their leader Onesilus, the brother of the king of Salamis, also

revolted. All the cities of the island of Cyprus joined the revolt except Amathus, as its population consisted of Pheonicians and Eteocypriots, the latter a clan who had lived on the island before the arrival of the Greeks. Eventually, Onesilus lay siege to Amathus but without success.

The suppression of the Ionian Revolt

Meanwhile, the Persians were preparing to deal a harsh lesson against the Ionian Revolt. According to their plan, they would first suppress the revolt in Cyprus, not only the most distant area that had revolted but also the most vulnerable one, as it lay near the Phoenician cities of Lebanon. The Phoenicians were attempting to use the opportunities created by the Ionian Revolt against the Greeks to promote their own commercial interests in the Mediterranean. The Persian plan was to deal with the cities of the Hellespont, with the Caria area being dealt with after Cyprus. The operations would then be completed with the subjugation of the cities of the western coast of Asia Minor that had constituted the initial core of the Ionian Revolt. The final part of the Persian plan was to be the capture of Miletus itself – the core of the revolt and the strongest, wealthiest city of the Aegean.

The Persians began putting their plan into operation by invading Cyprus. After their arrival on the island, the Persian army fought Onesilus near Salamis, managing to gain a victory, although not extinguishing the flames of revolt. The rebel Cypriot Greeks continued to resist, while the Ionian Greek fleet set sail for the island to offer its assistance. The Ionian fleet met the Persian one – mostly Pheonician ships – in the Gulf

of Salamis and defeated it. Despite the success in Cyprus, the situation took a negative turn in the Hellespont where the Persian general, Davrises, was able to retake the Greek cities. Subjugating Caria proved more difficult for the Persians as the Carians were excellent warriors and used weapons similar to those of the Greeks. It was to take the Persians two years and three hard-fought battles before they finally defeated the Carians in the autumn of 496 B.C., leaving Ionia as the only force opposing them. The satrap, Artaphernes, began its subjugation by attacking each city separately. At the end of 496 B.C., the Persians conquered the cities of Clazomenae and Cyme.

Aristagoras, understanding that defeat was near, realized that the time had come to save his own neck. He and a few of his followers fled to Myrcinus on the river Strymon, where he took refuge inside the fortified walls built earlier by Histiaeus. In late 496 B.C., he was slain by the Thracians during his siege of the city of Ennea Odoi. Meanwhile, Darius felt he could now use Histiaeus. The old tyrant of Miletus was now proven right, as he had forced the Persians to

send him back to Ionia, fulfilling his long-held desire to return. Initially, Histiaeus found himself at Sardis, but the satrap Arthaphernes suspected him of treachery, resulting in Histiaeus leaving the Persian camp and joining the rebels, to whom he contributed little substantial value. He then organized a pirate fleet that caused great depredation across the Aegean. His operations reached as far as Sicily where he fought against the Etruscans and Carthaginians. The Persians, in the meantime, took advantage of the Greeks' dispersion and subjugated many cities in succession, including Ephesus, the second-most important Ionian city after Miletus, which had by now been isolated.

In the spring of 494 B.C., the Persian forces surrounded Miletus to cut off its access from both land and sea. However, the Ionians and Aeolians continued to resist but decided not to risk a land battle against the Persians but to defend the city's seaward access. The Ionian fleet, consisting of 353 vessels, was drawn up along the coastline of the island of Lade, close to Miletus' harbor entrance. However, the Ionian and

The ruins of Ephesus, one of the largest Ionian cities. Its wealth and size were no help in avoiding Persian subjugation.

Aeolian crews refused to obey the orders of Admiral Dionysius of Phocia as they felt he was too strict in matters of discipline and also demanded constant training. The bickering among the various cities and the conspiracies of the exiled tyrants also contributed to slack discipline and a marked degeneration in the fighting abilities of the Greek fleet. The Persian fleet, comprised of 600 ships, mainly Phoenician ships along with some additional Egyptian, Cilician, and Cypriot vessels, faced the Greek fleet. In the summer of 494 B.C., the two fleets engaged in battle when the Phoenician ships moved suddenly against the Ionian vessels. During the clash, the Samians broke and fled, taking with them most of the Lesbian ships. Finally, the Greeks lost the naval battle and Admiral Dionysius was forced to flee, first to Cyprus, where, for a while, he attempted to continue the struggle, and later on to Sicily.

The defeat of the Greek fleet precipitated the fall of Miletus. The most important Greek city of the time was pillaged, plundered, and destroyed. The first target of the Persian looters was the rich temple of Apollo at Didyma, just as Hecateus had earlier prophesied when he had urged the Ionians to use its riches to secure their defense and freedom. The majority of the male population was killed, while the women and children were enslaved and sent off to the depths of Asia. A few years later, these deportees of the Ionian Revolt were used for the construction of the Royal Palace at Susa. Miletus was rebuilt in 479 B.C., after Ionia was liberated from Persian rule, but many centuries were to pass before it regained its former stature.

Following Miletus' fall, resistance by the remaining Ionian and Aeolian cities of the coast of Asia Minor and of the nearby islands seemed futile. By the close of 439 B.C., all pockets of resistance had been eradicated and the Aegean regions had returned to the status quo existing before the Ionian Revolt. Miltiades had been forced to leave his post as ruler of the Chersonesus area in Thrace and to return to Athens. During the revolution, he had sided with the Ionians and had captured the islands of Lemnos and Imbros, handing them over to Athens and thereby incurring Darius' wrath against the Athenians. The probable initiator of the revolt, Histiaeus, suffered a tragic end. The former tyrant still commanded a small fleet and attempted to attack the Phoenician ships sailing in the Aegean. He was caught and brought to the satrap Artaphernes, who hated him intensely and believed that if he sent him to Darius alive, the Persian king might remember the esteem he had felt for his old counselor and spare his life. So he ordered his men to kill him and had his head sent to Darius who, indeed, was displeased with this development. He ordered that Histiaeus be buried in such a manner as was fitting for a man who had offered great services to the king of Persia.

From then on, the Persians tried not to upset the inhabitants of the conquered Greek cities. The majority of the cities were allowed to retain the democratic forms of rule that had been created during the Ionian Revolt. Darius also believed that the blame for the revolt lay at the feet of the tyrants of the Ionian cities with their extravagant behavior. All fighting between the Greek cities was banned, and the Persian satrap of Sardis was designated as the authority to intervene and resolve any differences between them. In addition, taxation was not increased. The Persians, however, were under no illusion about the difficulty of controlling the Greek regions of the eastern Aegean coast as other free Greek cities lay quite near them. Darius and his counselors had learned from the Ionian Revolt that the Persian presence in the eastern Aegean would not be secure so long as there still existed free Greek cities on the coast of the western Aegean and at just a few days sailing from Ionia. The underlying Persian desire to punish the Athenians for their support of the Ionian Revolt was to lead to the Persian Wars of the future.

The Mardonius' expedition

The first opportunity to punish the Athenians came in 492 B.C., immediately following the suppression of the Ionian Revolt. The Persian goal was not merely the conquest of Athens but also to dominate the coastal areas of the northern Aegean. Despite the fact that the peoples of Thrace–with the exception of those living on the coast - had not taken part in the Ionian Revolt, the Persians had been obliged to abandon the region because they did not need the Thracian army to confront the Ionians and also because they had feared the Thracian garrisons would be isolated and annihilated. The man chosen to lead the campaign in Thrace was Mardonius, Darius' son-in-law. The Persian army and fleet gathered in Cilicia in the spring of 492 B.C. The fleet then sailed along the Ionian coastline, making a final show of force to the Greek coastal cities. While passing, Darius took care to oust many of the tyrannical governments of the Ionian cities as all the tyrants had, by this time, fallen out of his favor. The army crossed Asia Minor, passing by Sardis and ending in the Hellespont

The goddess Athena stands thoughtfully before a tombstone devoted to the Athenians who fell for their city. The sending of aid to the rebellious Greeks of Asia Minor was Athens' first attempt to expand its influence in the Aegean. (Athens, Acropolis Museum)

where the fleet lay anchored. In Thrace, the army attempted to defeat the many Thracian tribes of which only the Vryges resisted by means of a surprise attack on the Persian camp. During the attack, the Persians suffered heavy casualties, with Mardonius himself being wounded. Apart from these setbacks, the Vryges were eventually overcome and Mardonius advanced south. However, his march was to be cut short by the destruction of his fleet at Mt. Athos due to a terrific storm, during which, it is thought, 300 ships and 20,000 crewmen were lost. Following his fleet's destruction, Mardonius was forced to abandon the expedition, although the overall Persian plan remained unchanged. The main task for the Persian Empire remained the immediate and exemplary punishment of the Athenians - a move that would allow the Persians to establish their dominance in the Aegean.

Marathon, 490 B.C.
Athens crushes the Persian Might

The public assembly decision was final! The Athenians would fight within their city while waiting for the arrival of Spartan assistance. The Persian expeditionary force had arrived at Marathon and, encountering no resistance, had advanced on Athens. After a short siege, the Great King's hordes had breached the city walls and assaulted the city's interior, causing havoc and destruction. Athens no longer existed and, under its burnt ruins, western civilization, still in its infancy, lay buried. The city never lived to see the Golden Age of Pericles, and the rising star of its philosophers was extinguished before it had a chance to light the Europe's outposts. Yet, this is how history would have been written if, on that morning in August 490 B.C., the Athenian hoplites had not rushed to do battle against the invaders at Marathon.

Relations between city-states

Barely two years after Mardonius' campaign in northern Greece (492 B.C.), Darius stood ready to send a new expeditionary force against Athens and Eretria. The pretext of "punishing" the two cities for participating in the Ionian Revolt was a clever one, but it also helped those Greeks who wanted to break away into neutrality. Furthermore, many city-states would be very pleased and contented if the ambitious city of Athens were destroyed.

The foremost Greek powers of the period 510 B.C. to 490 B.C. were the city of Sparta with its Peloponnesian Alliance, a major military force at the time, the rapidly developing city of Athens, and the economically strong city of Corinth. There existed, of course, other sizeable city-states, for example Thebes. At this time, this city was still far from revealing its later ambition of uniting Boeotia under its rule. There was also Naxos, which ruled over a large area of the Cyclades islands and the island of Aegina, a developing naval power that competed with Athens for power. In addition, there was the city of Argos, which constantly challenged Sparta's leading position as a military power in control of the Peloponnesus. Within this general framework, some interesting relationships developed. First, a warm friendship had grown between Athens and Plataea, as the latter feared an increase in Theban power in Boeotia that would spell the end of its independence. On the other hand, a firm alliance had developed between Aegina and Thebes to counterbalance Athenian ambitions.

From 507 or 506 B.C., Aegina had been at war with Athens for the control of the Saronic Gulf, and its fleet had often raided the Attican coast. During the same period, Sparta and Argos were competing for dominance of the Cynouria region, while the Chalkidians and Eretrians had been enemies since the time of the Lelantine War. Thus, it does not seem so strange that Thebes, Aegina, and Argos sided with the Persians, as such

"The Dilemma,"
**painting by Christos
Giannopoulos.**

a move served their ambitions of dominating Greece.

Despite the fact that relations between Athens and Sparta had been tense following the Cleisthenes democratic reforms, the Spartans had often intervened on the side of Athens in its conflicts with Aegina. Furthermore, the Thebans had not hesitated to attack Athens as Aegina's allies. Analogous situations had occurred with other cities.

The start of the Persian Wars found the cities of Aegina, Chalkis, and Argos defeated and Thebes in alliance with the enemy. Athens and Sparta were the only cities remaining to bear the burden and share the dangers of the coming conflict.

Miltiades arrives in Athens

The ignominious end of the Ionian Revolt and the information that the Persians were making military preparations caused great unrest in Athens. The democrats were blamed for drawing the city into the Revolt, while a tendency to find scapegoats reveals how complex the situation was at the time.

A Persian guard. His weapons are a javelin and a bow. (Relief sculpture from the Palace of Persepolis)

At the start of spring 493 B.C., the tragic poet Phrynichus staged a play titled "The Fall of Miletus" in which he vividly described the collapse of the Ionian Revolt, causing it is said, the theatergoers to break into tears. The oligarchic faction, considered pro-Persian by many – although this is not verified by the facts – were extremely upset and took action, succeeding in having the playwright punished with a fine of 1,000 drachmas, on the premise that he had reminded the Athenians of "their own misfortunes." The play was then banned. While it could be true to say that the play reminded them of "their own misfortunes," it also promoted as correct and necessary support for the Ionians who had revolted. However, in those days there were few Athenians who believed their city could venture beyond its narrow confines and play an important role in the Aegean. On the contrary, public opinion held that bad politics had made them a direct Persian target. But, the democrats soon persuaded the flexible, ever-changing Athenian society that, since a Persian attack was a certainty, it would have to be resisted and that a powerful, popular leader was needed. So, in 493 B.C., Themistocles, a well-known young man from Phreattys and son of Neocles, who did not belong to the "nobles" class, was elected. Themistocles had predicted that a war with Persia was unavoidable. It also appears that he had already conceived a plan for a decisive engagement with the Persians at sea. This was a view Themistocles had not initially admitted in public as the Athenians did not want to make a stand against the Great King, though he had already managed to persuade his fellow citizens to spend the money emanating from the Laurion silver mines to construct the triremes that were required for the naval war against Aegina. The seagoing class of merchants, one of Athens' most democratic groups, eagerly supported Themistocles, a believer in constructing a fleet for the city's defense.

However, at that moment, the goddess Athena had chosen another man to protect her city, although the ambitious Themistocles was to become Athens' savior 10 years later. During the summer of 493 B.C., "with a sense of timing that was not at all theatrical" (P. Green: The Greco-Persian Wars), Miltiades arrived in Athens, bringing with him all his treasure and five triremes. He had fallen into disfavor with Darius for participating in the Ionian Revolt and for his conquest of Lemnos. Themistocles and Miltiades had nothing in common except a determination to fight, which would suffice for the time being. Miltiades was knowledgeable in Persian affairs and his constant fighting on the Thracian peninsula had matured him into an experienced war leader, a rare quality among the Athenians of the time.

Miltiades' opponents, whom Herodotus avoids naming, brought him to trial under the accusation that, in Chersonesus, he had behaved like a tyrant. His aristocratic origins, the fact that Peisistratus and Hippias had awarded him the Chersonesus post, and his cooperation with the Persians were his political opponents' primary evidence against him. However, Miltiades' integrity, financial strength, fame for his efforts to destroy the Danube bridge during Darius' campaign against Scythia, plus the fact that his opponents used untrustworthy people to testify against him all contributed to his being declared innocent. In addition, during the 491 B.C. elections, he was elected as one of the 10 generals, in company with his friend and supporter Aristides. "Sometimes the people elected better men than they could imagine." (P. Green: The Greco-Persian Wars)

In the meantime, ever-more frequent reports of Persian military preparations had made it clear that the city's defenses had to be readied without delay. Themistocles, an avid believer in the concept that the war had to be fought at sea, proposed fortifying Piraeus, abandoning Athens, and placing all hopes in a decisive naval battle. As expected, the city's oligarchic and aristocratic factions forcefully opposed this plan of action. The city's aristocratic cliques depended on the incomes from their estates, abandoning them would spell financial disaster following any pillaging by the invaders. The farmers and, indeed, all those who possessed a strong feeling for the defense of the

A bust of Herodotus. The "Father of History" is the primary source for the Persian Wars.

homeland, the family, and their ancestors' honor sided with the aristocrats. Themistocles had to battle against the great weight of tradition, which eventually forced him not to persevere with his views. In 492 B.C., his naval construction plan was shelved, despite the fact that the Public Assembly had voted for the fortifying of Piraeus. The Athenians decided to remain and defend the land of their forefathers. Themistocles' star was destined to shine not at Marathon but at Salamis. For the time being, he would stand in the hoplite phalanx shoulder-to-shoulder with Miltiades and Aristides. Faced with the Persian threat, there was no time left for disagreements. The two opposing sides made peace and began to prepare the defenses. It appears that only the followers of the Peisistatids were left out of the whole affair concerning the city's survival.

THE CAMPAIGN AGAINST ATHENS 490 B.C.

Map illustration by Christos Giannopoulos / PERISCOPIO PUBLICATIONS

Legend:
- Persian forces
- Platean infantry
- Athenian infantry
- Athenian colonists' infantry
- Battles or sieges

The Persian expedition

According to Herodotus, in the spring of 491 B.C., Darius sent envoys to the Aegean islands and to all the cities of mainland Greece demanding "earth and water" as a sign of submission. The islanders, first among them being the inhabitants of Thasos, immediately succumbed to the Persian demand, followed by Aegina, famous for its ships, and the cities of northern Greece. The Athenians considered the Aeginetan reaction to be very dangerous. Until that moment, these two competing cities had been able to wage war with each other in a manner that was controlled and balanced, but the thought of possible aid from Persia would lead to a major upset of the balance of power in the region. The Athenians asked Sparta for assistance and accused the Aeginetans of being "traitors of Greece." Furthermore, they threw Darius' envoys, who had been sent to request "earth and water," into a deep ditch, with the envoys to Sparta also suffering the same fate. According to the words of the "Father of History" Herodotus, "the first (the Athenians) threw into a ditch those who came to ask for earth and water and the second (the Spartans) threw them into a deep well and called to them to get earth and water from there and take it to their king." However, Herodotus' information about the envoys being sent throughout Greece does not seem accurate, as the sole purpose of the Persian campaign was to exact punishment on Naxos, Eretria, and Athens, not the submission of all Greece, at least not at this early stage. If there had been any Persian diplomatic activity in the Greek world before the Battle of Marathon, its aim would have been to isolate Athens from the other city-states and not to demand the submission of all the cities. In addition, as will be seen, the numerical size of the Persian expeditionary force was insufficient for the subjugation of all mainland Greece. While Darius' diplomatic gestures are not known, the possibility cannot be ruled out that the Athenians faced the Marathon invaders almost alone (with the exception of the Plataeans) as a result of successful Persian diplomacy.

In the spring of 490 B.C., the Persian army gathered on Cilicia's Plain of Aleion. Herodotus does not state an exact number but merely writes, "Many well-armed men gathered." Herodotus' lack of information has created a plethora of calculations on the part of later historians. The epigram writer Simonides calculates that the Persians fielded 200,000 men, while Plato mentions 500,000 and Justinus 600,000. Pausanias, conservatively, put forward an estimate of 300,000. These figures all appear somewhat

overstated, but this could be because ancient writers usually included in their estimates not only soldiers but also oarsmen, technicians, slaves, and many others. Bousolt and Glotz estimate the Persian army at 50,000, while H. Bengtson offers a figure of just 20,000, which seems too low. N.G.L. Hammond writes of a force of 80,000 men, including 25,000 soldiers. Meanwhile, other researchers base their figures on the number of ships (600) and arrive at combined figures of soldiers and sailors ranging from 130,000 to 150,000. Some diminish the total expedition force to a number between 30,000 and 55,000 men. Hammond's estimate would appear to be closest to the truth. If, however, we try to calculate the number of men on the basis of each ship's capacity and then add the large volumes of cargo, including arms, provisions, and other materials, it then appears logical that the Persians would have numbered between 30,000 and 50,000 troops, with a further 70,000 to 90,000 sailors. A conservative estimate, taking into account possible losses during the conquest of Naxos and Eretria and the number of men left behind to guard the conquered Aegean islands, would be that between 30,000 to 40,000 Persians faced the Athenians at Marathon.

So, whatever way one looks at it, the truth remains that the number of invaders far exceeded that of defenders.

As for the number of ships, Herodotus mentions 600 triremes. It is certain that the majority of the ships were transports. If we accept Herodotus' figure, then it is logical to assume that from 400 to 450 of these vessels were transports with the remainder being warships.

The Persian noble Datis, an old warrior and an officer from the

An Athenian polemarch, 490 B.C.
The composite breastplate (cuirass) of
prominent Athenian citizens was lined
with different-sized, overlapping bronze
scales, while the sides of some sections
were painted with vivid decorative
patterns. This officer's Corinthian
helmet is in two colors – the dome is left
in bronze natural color while the facial
section has been painted black for the
purpose of personal identification. The
helmet's tall crest holder adds height to
the polemarch, while his shield's metal
covering is decorated with a white bull's
head – the favored emblem of particular
Athenian clans recalling the memory the
legend of Theseus' fight with the large
white bull of Marathon. (uniform
research and reconstruction
by Christos Giannopoulos)

An Athenian hoplite, 490 B.C. This particular
warrior represents a typical Athenian hoplite
from the lower classes that fought at Marathon.
He wears an Attican-style crested helmet, light
leather wings, long bronze greaves, and is
carrying a "hoplon" type shield, the face of
which has a woolen cloth attached to protect the
legs from Persian arrows (some infantrymen
used leather aprons for the same purpose). His
offensive weapons are the long thrusting spear
and the thrusting-slashing sword (not shown
here). (uniform research and reconstruction
by Christos Giannopoulos)

generation that had destroyed Ninevi and who, possibly, had participated in the suppression of the Ionian Revolt, and the Persian Artaphernes, the king's nephew and son of the satrap of Sardis of the same name, were the two commanders of the expeditionary force. The old, former tyrant Hippias participated in the expeditionary force as an advisor. The Persian leaders believed that his presence would weaken the Athenian defenses, as the followers of the Peisistratids would then play the role of the fifth phalanx.

A statuette of a warrior, possibly Spartan, from Dodoni (530-510 B.C.). In the years preceding the Persian Wars, Sparta's military power was the greatest in all Greece. (Archeological Museum of Ioannina)

In the summer of 490 B.C., the Persian triremes set sail for the Aegean with orders to execute the commands of the Great King, namely "to conquer Athens and Eretria and to fetch before him their inhabitants as slaves." The Persians did not follow Mardonius' plan of the 492 B.C. expedition that had provided for combined action by the army and navy. The destruction of the fleet at Mt. Athos had discouraged them to such an extent that they now decided not to enter Greece via the northern route, but to approach their target by crossing the Aegean.

The Persian ships sailed past Ionia to Samos. From there, the fleet headed for Naxos and launched a surprise attack. The Naxians had no time to organize their defense and were quickly overcome. The island was pillaged, the temples and houses burned, and those Naxians who did not manage to escape to the mountains were taken prisoner. When the inhabitants of

Delos were informed of the Naxos disaster, they abandoned the island and fled to Tinos. Datis, however, requested them to return with the promise that he would never harm the island on which Apollo and Artemis had been born. He even made an impressive sacrifice to the Delia Apollo, burning 300 talents worth of incense on his altar. By this gesture, Persian propaganda tried to dissuade the Greeks from resisting the invaders on the pretense that their sole goal was to punish Eretria and Athens. By a diabolical coincidence, as if nature itself wished to denounce the Persian overtures, a strong earthquake shook the area and destroyed Delos. The Persian triremes then headed northwest through the Cyclades, conscripting men by force on the way, and arrived at Carystos, the southernmost city of Euboea, where they came face to face with the locals' refusal to surrender. In consequence, the Persians besieged their city and began burning the crops in the surrounding countryside. This left the Carystians no other choice but to surrender. The Persians' next target was the city of Eretria. Doubt and confusion reigned in Eretria at the time. Some Eretrians wanted to negotiate with the invaders, while others proposed abandoning the city and hiding in the nearby heights from where they could launch surprise attacks against the enemy. The Eretrians asked the Athenians for assistance and were sent 2,000 of their compatriots (some writers state 4,000 men) who owned estates on Chalkis. Aeschynes, the son of Nothon, a prominent citizen of Eretria, informed the Athenian troops that the situation in the city was pitiable due to internal bickering and advised them to leave. After listening to him, the Athenians departed, crossing over to the mainland town of Oropos. The Eretrians, on the brink of a civil war, decided to defend themselves from inside the city walls. After just six days of siege, Eretria fell due to an act of treason. Two prominent citizens, Euphorbus and Philagrus, the son of Acauneus, handed their city to the enemy and the Persians burned it to the ground. The inhabitants were taken prisoner, sold into slavery, and deported to Arderrica, near Susa, as punishment for the destruction of Sardis. A few days later, according to Herodotus, "the Persians set sail with their ships for the coasts of Attica, exerting great pressure on the way and believing that they would do to the Athenians what they had done to the Eretrians." The Athenians also entertained the same thoughts: The invaders would not content themselves with a mere declaration of submission but would destroy their city. The barbarism exhibited by the Persians in Eretria removed all basis of argument from those Athenians who continued to support the notion of cooperation as the best solution. After the destruction of the Euboean city, the Athenians thought their turn had come. Therefore, they had to fight and exhaust all possibilities left to them in order to save their city and themselves.

The Persian ships sailed between the straits of Euboea and Attica. Their immediate destination was the plain of Marathon, around 42 kilometers to the northeast of Athens, on the coast opposite Eretria. It was here that the decisive battle was to take place. At this juncture, we should remind ourselves that the birthplace of what is today called Western Civilization was the city of Athens. It will then be appreciated that, on the outcome of this battle depended not only the fate of Athens but also the future of Europe.

The topography of Marathon

The Marathon plain stretches along the coastline of Dacria, an area bordered by the peninsula of Kynosoura to its northeast. It was formed by alluvial sediment, and has a total length of 9 kilometers, with a maximum width of 3 kilometers. The plain is surrounded on three sides (southern, western, and northern) by mountains that are a continuation of the Mt. Pendeli range. Its eastern side rests on the sea. To be more specific, the following mountains, Stavrokoraki to the north, Kotroni to the west, and Agrieliki to the south, border the area. At the time of the battle, the greater part of the plain's northeastern area, between Mt. Stavrokoraki and Kynosoura, was covered by a large swamp, the "Great Swamp." Pausanias calls it "a very swampy lake" (Pausanias: On Attica, 32, 7). A smaller swamp, the "Small Swamp" lay to the southwest, between the beach and Agrieliki (the area called Valaria). In the center of the plain, and to the southwest of the Great Swamp, was the River Charadrus, while in the southwestern area of the swamp there was a water source named Makaria. The section toward the promontory edge of the bay, the coastal area of Schinias, was covered by a forest. Two roads lead from the Marathon plain to Athens. The first road heads east, passing through the city of Pallene and between Mt. Hymettus and Mt. Pendeli. The second, a smaller mountain

A Roman copy of the bust of Miltiades (approximately 450 B.C.). Despite the fact that his arrival in Athens caused dissention among the citizenry, it soon became clear that he was the only man capable of neutralizing the Persian danger. (Ravenna, National Museum)

THE MARATHON PLAIN
490 B.C.

Tricorythos

Mt Stavrokoraki

Macaria Springs

Mt Drakonera

The Great Marsh

Lake Stomi

Mt Kotroni

Charadros?

Shoinias Beach

Dakria beach

Kynosoyra

Probalinthos

Sacred Groove

Herakleion?

Marathon

MARATHON BAY

Cape Marathon

Mt Agrieliki

Valaria territory

Vrexiza Marsh

N

W

E

S

A map of the Marathon Area.

road, passes through the modern town of Kifissia and then forks, with one branch leading to today's Marathon from one side, and the other leading to Marathon through today's village of Vrana.

According to Herodotus, it was Hippias who had proposed Marathon as a first line of defense as the plain was suitable for cavalry action. Herodotus calls it "a perfect area of Attica for using horses." It may also be that the short distance to Eretria played an important role in the choice of an embarkation point for the invaders. It is also possible that Hippias wished to repeat his father Peisistratus' triumphal march through Eretria and Marathon, when he had established his tyranny. In addition,

the poor farmers of the region were faithful followers of the Peisistratids. Another consideration is that the Persian leaders thought, if the Athenians rushed to Marathon to stop them, the tyrannical faction would take the opportunity to seize the city. However, the majority of students of the battle are of the view that Datis needed the perfect space that Marathon readily provided for deploying his cavalry. One of the historians, P. Green, shares the same view, writing that Datis needed space to use his horsemen and Marathon offered the perfect conditions, as it was a long strip of land between the mountains and the sea which afforded easy access to Athens via the passage between the two mountains, Hymettus

A Persian, or Mede high-ranking officer, fifth century B.C. The illustrated polemarch wears luxurious armor made of gold plated scales and decorated with sun disks, a fact that brings to mind the phrase in ancient Greek literature of the "golden-clad Medes." All items of his outfit (cloth tiara tied under his chin, long-sleeved tunic, wide breeches with purple strips, leather boots and large arrow case containing both the bow and its arrows) is indicative of the pure Medic culture, while his golden decorations (around the neck and wrists) reveal that he is a man of a high social standing who was part of the King's entourage. His offensive weapons are the bow, the long slashing sword, the short akinakes sword, and the Iranian wedge-shaped ax known as a "sagaris." (uniform research and reconstruction by Christos Giannopoulos)

and Pendeli. In addition, Herodotus also stated that the Persians selected Marathon "because the area was suitable for maneuvering cavalry." There is also another, opposing view: The area's extensive swamps and the River Charadrus that bisected the plain was not suitable for cavalry. The area was "irregular, unsuitable ground for horses, full of mud, lakes, and stagnant water." (Commentaries, Plato's Menexenus 240c) It would appear that it was possible that the Persians chose Marathon as a base of operations, not because they wanted to use their cavalry but to entice the Athenians away from their poorly defended capital and so attack it with part of their forces and, in this way, capture the city. If, indeed, the Persian commanders had made such a plan, then the absence of Persian cavalry during the battle can be explained. It could be surmised that the cavalry had been sent off on some secret mission. Our own conclusion is that it was Hippias who chose Marathon as the battleground.

The Persians landed on the sandy beach of Schinias, on the northeastern edge of Marathon bay, between the Great Swamp and the peninsular promontory of Kynosoura. At this point, there was sufficient protection from a landward attack, an easy way of retreat toward the sea, and plenty of grassland for their horses. The Persian encampment was probably set up near Tricorynthos (present-day village of Kato Souli), between the Charadrus River and the Great Swamp. Datis and Artaphernes, having landed at dawn, lost no time in organizing the defense of the road that led north, toward Ramnous, while their cavalry scouts were sent off to carry out an inspection of the plain. There was no doubt that the Persians had chosen a strong position. The omens, however, were

bad. A legend of the kind that usually predetermines an outcome says that Hippias sneezed so hard when he set foot on Marathon that one of his teeth fell out. After looking in vain for it in the sand, he muttered to himself "After all, the land is not ours; and we shall never be able to bring it under our thrall. All my share in it is the portion of which my tooth has possession."

The critical moments

The signal fire was lit on top of Mt. Pendeli to warn the Athenians that the enemy forces had landed. A runner, perhaps Pheidipides, was immediately sent to Sparta to seek help. Herodotus gives us his words to the Persian ephors: "Men of Lacedaemon, the Athenians beseech you to hasten to their aid, and not allow that state, which is the most ancient in all Greece, to be enslaved by the barbarians. Eretria, look you, is already carried away captive; and Greece weakened by the loss of an important city." The Spartans expressed their desire to help, but added that they were unable to give it to them until the next full moon. (One wonders if they would have said the same thing if the Persians had landed on the banks of the Eurotas River?) They also explained that if they sent troops now, they would break their established religious law. This law was connected with the Karneia religious festival, which was held in honor of Apollo. They added that, "it was then the ninth day month; and they could not march out of Sparta on the ninth as the moon had not yet reached its fullness." The modern reader may see all this as an obvious excuse. P. Green describes the religious pretensions of the Spartans with subtle irony: "No doubt the Spartans were honestly

An illustration of an Athenian hoplite from the end of the sixth century B.C. Inscribed plaque from the Acropolis of Athens. (Athens, Acropolis Museum)

religious and established traditionalists. We have no right, in the lack of strong evidence to the contrary, to accuse them of showing a religious hypocrisy for political reasons. However, it is doubtless strange to observe how often such religious taboos of theirs perfectly fitted their practical plans." Despite all this, the Spartans placed an expeditionary force on a war footing, and kept it ready to move when the moon allowed or the battle called.

At this point, it is easy to begin questioning the Spartans' motives as, on the one hand, they had rejected the Persian demands outright and in a nonforgiving way, while on the other they would not help Athens at that critical moment. This strange Lacedaemonian foreign policy reflected the opposite natures of the royal party that, with Cleomenes I as its representative always followed a policy of expansion and hegemony, and the ephors that were constantly trying to curtail royal powers.

Cleomenes, knowing that Persian aid to the island of Aegina would upset the balance of power in the Saronic gulf and the Peloponnesus (and that many cities might ally with Aegina and the Persians after a possible destruction of Athens), had already sent an expeditionary force to the island once before, in 491 B.C. At that time, Argos had sent 1,000 hoplites to aid the Aeginetans' defense, but the islanders signed a treaty with the Spartans, as they knew they had no hope of defeating them. The outcome was that the Persians lost an

An Elite Saca Archer, 500 - 480 B.C. The Saca archers were the elite allied units of the Empire's infantry, the equivalent of the Roman "auxilia" units. They were particularly capable and could even fight as shock troops. Apart from their bow, they were also equipped with other offensive weapons, including a curved sword and the wedge-shaped "sagaris" ax, which could penetrate all types of Greek helmet and cuirasses. The Sacas' uniform's national identity was the leopard-skin cap with its pointed top from which some of their tribal names were derived, such as "Saka Tigrakhauda," meaning "the Sacas with the pointed caps." In the ancient world it was strongly rumored that their clothing and padded cuirasses were made from human skin. (uniform research and reconstruction by Christos Giannopoulos)

A Plataean Warrior, 500-490 B.C. This particular illustration is based on depictions of warriors on items of pottery excavated from the Plateaens' tomb at Marathon. It appears that most Plataean warriors were aged between 15 and 25, and, strangely, are depicted wearing long mantles when they fought. They wore undecorated Corinthian helmets, long bronze greaves, and carried shields of the "hoplon" or Boeotian "thyreos" types (these can also be seen on some of depictions of Athenian hoplites of the period). (uniform research and reconstruction by Christos Giannopoulos)

important, strategic foothold on Aegina, which they could otherwise have used for the attack on the Athenians, for which they had been preparing. Indeed, a year later when the Athenians were facing the Persians at Marathon, the Aeginetans remained totally inactive. Herodotus recognizes the importance of the Spartan intervention in Aegina when he mentions that by attacking Aegina, Cleomenes "was working for the good of Greece."

The Spartan ephors feared that Cleomenes' latest victory would increase his power such as the earlier defeat of the Argives in Seteia in 494 B.C. had done. To this end, the ephors organized themselves to try to depose him and, by various nefarious means, managed to have him exiled. One of these was by accusing him of having bribed the Delphic Oracle to gain confirmation of Demaratus' illegal birth, an event leading to Demaratus losing his office. Thus Sparta, without the capable hand of Cleomenes, would not respond to the Athenian call for aid when the Persians landed at Marathon. Herodotus also mentions that, around the same time, the Spartans were having problems with a helot uprising. Spartan reluctance to answer the Athenian calls for assistance was further aggravated by the Arcadian raids, which the exiled Cleomenes had led to revolt. Many contemporary historians and researchers think that Sparta did not go into action because of considerations of strategy. If Persia dealt a severe blow to Athens, the city's power and influence would stagnate. At this point, the Spartans would intervene to prevent its total destruction, but would also force it to follow its policies. The Spartan ephors believed that a small war in terms of geographical expansion ("limited

war") between the Athenians and the Persians might obtain the results they themselves had failed to achieve against the dangerous, democratic city of Athens. This view is further supported by the fact that the Spartan expeditionary force sent to Athens arrived at Marathon two or three days after the battle. Herodotus points out "their haste to arrive in time was so great that they covered the distance from Sparta to Athens in only three days." This means that they had started their march on the actual day of the Battle of Marathon, in the certain knowledge that a limited blow against Athens had already been struck and what now was to be avoided was its total submission. However, the Spartans in no way expected an Athenian victory.

Another aspect of this line of argument is that the small number of just 2,000 men of the Spartan expeditionary force appears to have been specifically conceived as reinforcements for the Athenians, and not to free the city of a possible siege in case the Athenian army was defeated at Marathon. It can, of course, be added that Sparta was so thinly populated that it never possessed enough troops to be able to send a larger force to Athens, as it always had to retain enough men to counter any threat in its own region. Plato, in his "Laws," talks not only of the revolution of the helots but also mentions military clashes with the Messenians who forced the Spartans to maintain an army in their area. What is certain, however, is that as the Spartans had decided on sending 2,000 hoplites to the area, they could have sent them earlier.

From the moment the news of the fall of Eretria reached Athens, intense disagreement sprang up among Athenians. The 10 generals who headed the Athenian army were divided as to how they should act. Some among them supported the view that as they were outnumbered, it would be suicide to wage battle in open country and, instead, proposed a defense in the city. Others, with Miltiades as their chief spokesman, insisted on fighting the Persians on the Marathon plain, with the army drawn up facing them. Their arguments appeared persuasive. There were no strong walls protecting the city, as the famous Long Walls had not yet been built. Also, there was no connection with Phaleron on the shoreline where there was still a harbor, and Athens had not yet built a fleet capable of assuring the supply of provisions in the case of a long siege. It also seemed doubtful that the Spartan expeditionary force would be able to break through the Persian siege ring around Athens and assist those in the city. Finally, with the Eretrian misfortunes still fresh in everyone's mind, no one could guarantee that the hand of a traitor would not open the city gates to the enemy. In addition, Miltiades had great confidence in the training, fighting ability, and the better weapons of the Greek hoplite. The Ionians' fatal mistake of shutting themselves inside the city walls and never facing the enemy on open ground – even when the enemy had insufficient cavalry forces – should not be repeated. The Greek phalanx would have better chances on open ground. Miltiades had good reason to believe that postponing the events would also engender a defeatist attitude that would harm the citizens' morale. If that happened, the pro-Persian group would attempt to take advantage of the negative situation and put themselves forward as mediators between besiegers and besieged to negotiate a "surrender" of

the city to the enemy. Indeed, the opposite effect would occur if defense from within the city were not adopted: Entering into battle with the enemy on the open field would boost the Athenian morale.

The strategic advantages of making a stand at Marathon were significant. The plain offered just a small area of its expanse for use by the Persian cavalry, but was eminently suitable for the warriors of the Greek phalanx and for the full deployment of the hoplites, with this alone increasing the chances of victory. The deployment of the army would also protect from destruction the townships of Marathon and Oenoe and all of the surrounding areas, up to the Athens' city limits. The appearance of the Athenian hoplites in the area would also prevent any pro-Persian activities among Hippias' followers.

At such a critical moment for the city's future, the words of Miltiades to the polemarch, Callimachus, proved crucial for the final decision. Herodotus gives us the words of Miltiades: "Callimachus, it is now in your hands to enslave Athens or make her free, and thereby leave behind for all posterity a memorial such as not even Harmodius and Aristogeiton left. Now the Athenians have come to their greatest danger since they first came into being, and, if we surrender, it is clear what we will suffer when handed over to Hippias. But, if the city prevails, it will take first place among Hellenic cities. I will tell you how this can happen, and how the deciding voice on these matters has devolved upon you. The 10 generals are of divided opinion, some urging to attack, others urging not to. If we do not attack now, I expect that great strife will fall upon, and shake the spirit of the Athenians, leading them to side with the Persians. But, if we attack now, before anything unsound corrupts the Athenians, we can win the battle, if the gods are fair. All this concerns and depends on you and in this way: If you vote with me, your country will be free and your city the first in Greece. But, if you side with those eager to avoid battle, you will have the opposite to all the good things I enumerated." (Herodotus, 6, 109) Callimachus agreed, and the Athenians, motivated by Miltiades' good reputation, decided to face the Persians at Marathon – a decision to which, according to tradition, Aristides also made a positive contribution.

The Marathon force probably included 9,000 elite hoplites, 900 from each tribe. This number appears small when compared to the magnitude of the threat facing them, and seems even smaller when we take into account the writings of many

This illustration is based on a sculpture of a Greek archer from the western pediment of the Temple of Aphaia on the island of Aegina. The Aeginetans ultimately became one of the Athenians' most implacable enemies. (illustration by Romilos Fronimidis)

historians who state that Athens, during that period, was in a position to field from 25,000 to 30,000 lightly armed hoplites and horsemen. It must be supposed that not a negligible percentage of the population (of the poorer classes, obviously) would refuse to participate in the battle, as they desired the return of Hippias to power. In addition, guarding the city against a possible Persian siege and also against a possible, but real danger of the tyrant's supporters precipitating an uprising required a force of at least 6,000-8,000 hoplites. Also, it cannot be ruled out that there was a possibility that the Athenian generals calculated that, in the event of a defeat, the size of the guard was sufficient to defend the city against a siege until the Spartan military aid arrived.

Yet another possibility is that Miltiades submitted his proposal to the Public Assembly as a "psephisma" (decree) for sanction by vote, but the original text has not survived. From later sources, there is information that there existed in the fourth century B.C. a psephisma by Miltiades, although its authenticity has been questioned. Herodotus mentions nothing about it. Sometimes, however, the myth is more attractive than historical reality and, thus, leads us to the Pnyx where the Public Assembly sanctioned the order to "take your provisions and advance." The Athenians put on their armor, bid their wives farewell, and went to meet their destiny.

Persian shield bearer file-leader (Sparabara) 500-490B.C. The Sparabara constituted the first line of armored strike troops of the Persian infantry whose task it was to protect the rear rank bowmen while they launched their arrows in mass volleys against an attacking enemy. Their clothing and composite shield (made of cane and leather) featured decorative patterns of Eurasian origin and style, and indicated either the unit to which they belonged or the geographical region from where they had been conscripted. For offensive weapons, the shield-bearer carried a lance with a strong, round base and the distinctive Iranian short sword (akinakes). A padded (akheton) linen cuirass attached by leather shoulder strips protects his body. (uniform research and reconstruction by Christos Giannopoulos)

The date of the battle

One of the basic questions any student of the Battle of Marathon encounters is the precise dating of the battle. Herodotus, our basic source, states that the runner sent by the Athenians to seek Spartan help took two days to arrive. The Spartans, as stated earlier, declared they could not send aid as it was the ninth day of the month (the month is not specified), and they could not undertake military action before the arrival of the full moon on the 15th of the month. Plutarch says the date of the battle was the 6th of October, which coincides with the Artemis festival in Athens. He also adds that on that date each year, the Athenians began to sacrifice 500 young goats to Artemis as a gesture of gratitude. Modern historians, however, reject Plutarch's date, believing that the Boetian history writer was led astray by the sacrifice of gratitude, and support the view that the battle must have surely occurred before the 6th of October.

Returning to Herodotus, he states that the runner was ordered to go to Sparta as soon as news of the Persians' arrival at Marathon became known, and that he arrived on the ninth of the month after a two-day run. The Spartans, on the other hand, set out after the full moon, that is on the 15th or 16th of the month. The months of antiquity were based on the moon's phases. The Spartans arrived at Marathon three days later, around the 18th or 19th of the month. If we assume that the runner left for Sparta as soon as news of the Persian invasion was known, and that it took him two days to arrive, then the Persians must have landed on the coast on the 7th of the month. If we now take into consideration the fact that each general was given the leadership of the army for one day, then the battle took place on the sixth day, i.e., on the 14th or 15th of the month, as Miltiades was the leading general of the sixth tribe in the order (Oeneis). This date seems the most probable, although yet another problem now arises. When the Spartans arrived in Athens – on the 18th or 19th of the month, four or five days after the battle – they asked to see the dead Persians: "... they demanded to see the Medes. They were then led to Marathon and saw them there." However, it seems very strange that the Athenians had not buried their dead opponents by then as the temperatures were high, the battle having taken place in August or September, and the risk of epidemic diseases was high. Plato indirectly solves this matter by stating that the Spartans arrived in Athens the day after the battle, but his testimony cannot be confirmed.

Ancient sources make no mention of the month of the battle, with the result that modern researchers have resorted to some interesting calculations. The date of the battle is connected with the full moon of either the 10th of August (the 15th of Hekatombion) or the ninth of September (the 15th of Metageitnion) or the eighth of October (the 15th of Boedromion). One logical supposition is that the battle happened in September (Metageitnion), as this month corresponded with the month called "Karneion" in Sparta, which coincides with the Karneia festival that the Spartans had used as an excuse not to send aid to Athens. Herodotus, however, says nothing about the Karneia festival, although he mentions limitations of a similar nature in his account of the Thermopylae battle: "... it was not possible to send aid immediately as this was against traditional custom. It was the 9th day of the month then and they said they could not start their expedition on that day as it was not a day of full moon."

As far as the month of October (Boedromion) is concerned, it seems unlikely that one can accept this time as the date, as it is difficult to accept that the Persian fleet, that had sailed from Cilicia in the summer, had taken four months to arrive in Marathon Bay, even if it had been delayed by battles in Naxos and Eretria. In the end, the most probable month for the Battle of Marathon is August (Hekatombion), although September cannot be ruled out entirely.

The Athenians' arrival at Marathon

According to Attic Mythology, a fierce battle was fought between the Argives and the Athenians at Marathon, when the latter refused to give King Eurystheus the children of Heracles who had sought refuge at Marathon. Before the battle, an oracle had been consulted that stated that the Athenians would win if they sacrificed a woman of noble descent. Makaria, the daughter of Heracles and Deianera, whose name had been given to a nearby water spring, volunteered herself. The Athenians and Heracleides defeated the Argives and killed Eurystheus. Grateful for the favorable outcome of the battle, the Athenians built a sanctuary in honor of Heracles – the famous Heracleion temple. As Herodotus informs us, the Athenians camped near the Heracleion temple, reaching the area by taking the safe road from Kifissia.

The sanctuary is located in the area of Valaria, north of the Little Swamp and near the ruins of the ancient church of St. Theodorus. However, it seems likely that on the day of the battle the Athenians finally chose to make their stand on the northeastern

The beach as Schinias. This was where the Persian expeditionary force landed. (photo of "Ekdotiki of Athens")

*Persian spear bearers.
Their weapons consisted
of a large shield and a
spear. (relief sculpture
from Persepolis)*

occupation of the position at
Heracleion, shouts of joy were heard
from their camp. The great army of
the Plataeans (1,000 hoplites,
according to Herodotus) "went there
to reinforce them and help with all
their forces." Commanded by
Arimnestus, they had come to fight at
the allies' side and to share in the glory
or die.

Miltiades' plans for the battle

The main staff body of the
Athenian army was the "Military
Council," which, in this case,
comprised the polemarch,
Callimachus, and the 10 generals, one
from each tribe. The generals were
given operational command by
rotation, which amounted to a
different general each day, who acted
as the leading general or second-in-
command under the polemarch. The
polemarch, according to ancient
tradition, was the supreme
commander. In this particular case,
however, the four generals, who had
supported the decision before the
Public Assembly to stand at Marathon,
ceded their place to Miltiades: "The
generals who favored battle
surrendered their lot of leadership to
Miltiades each time it was their turn to
lead." (Herodotus, 6, 110) P.Green
makes this acute observation: "It was a
pleasant moment when the democratic
principles retreated and gave their
place to superior technical
knowledge." The fine example was
first set by Aristides, who, as Plutrach
says, "when his turn came to lead, he
gave his place to Miltiades, teaching
the generals that obeying and
following those who think correctly is
not humiliating, but is honest and can
save lives. Thus, having eradicated the
competition among the generals, and

slopes of Mt. Agrieliki as from there,
they could examine the movements of
the Persian infantry and could also
easily defend themselves from a
possible enemy cavalry attack. If,
instead, they had remained at
Heracleion, they would have run the
risk of being outflanked by Persian
forces that would move in from the
Vranas area. In addition, if they made
their stand in the central area of the
mountainous regions on the western
side of the plain, not far from the most
likely area of where the battle would
take place (i.e. the high, flat ground
between the two swamps), the
Athenians realized they would be able
to launch an immediate counterattack
when they thought the right moment
arrived. Toward the end of the first
day, or the early morning of the next
day, following the Athenians'

having urged them to adopt one opinion, the best one, he strengthened Miltiades' position that now, without any further obstacles, had total control. This was because all the generals, having given up their daily generalships, now obeyed Miltiades' orders."

More recent opinion (U.Wilcken) states that the generalship was awarded to Miltiades by Public Assembly vote – a possibility that seems unlikely in the ever – suspicious climate of Athenian democracy.

Whatever the case, Herodotus states that Miltiades accepted the offer of command but waited for the day of his own generalship in order to do battle, wishing, perhaps, to take all the responsibility for the operation, whatever the outcome. Despite this, the polemarch had to agree, and this explains why Miltiades set out to persuade Callimachus with his argument. Callimachus, who was the supreme commander, agreed with Miltiades that the battle should be fought at Marathon and then left him free to decide the timing of the plan's execution.

Miltiades had to solve three serious problems: the enemy's numerical superiority, the presence of the Persian cavalry, and the presence of enemy archers.

In order to face the enemy's numerical superiority, Miltiades had to make certain that the fighting was conducted man-to-man, with the hoplite phalanx solid and deployed. If the Athenians managed to make contact with the Persians, then the battle plan, their excellent training, and their superior weaponry would give them a high chance of victory. However, what impeded immediate contact for a man-to-man battle, with a distance of 5-7 kilometers between the two armies, were the Persian cavalry and archers. These could seriously upset the close ranks of the phalanx before it had a chance to strike at the enemy ranks. To counteract any such move, Miltiades ordered obstacles made of wood beams onto which sharpened wooden sticks were fixed along their length at right angles. With the use of these obstacles, Miltiades could protect the phalanx's flanks from the menacing Persian cavalry.

One or two days after the Athenians appeared at Marathon, the Persians, having first made spasmodic moves on the flanks to draw their opponents into battle, redeployed to an advanced position by the

An Assyrian-style bronze Persian helmet, part of the spoils from the Battle of Marathon, dedicated to Zeus at Olympia and bearing the inscription "To Zeus from the Athenians, who took it from the Medes." (Archeological Museum of Olympia)

ORGANIZATION AND TERMINOLOGY OF THE PERSIAN CENTURY

(Uniform research and reconstruction-illustration: Christos Giannopoulos)

Satabam (century)

Pascadathapatis (rear file leader - adjutant to the decarch file leader)

Dathaba (decarchy - squad of 10 men)

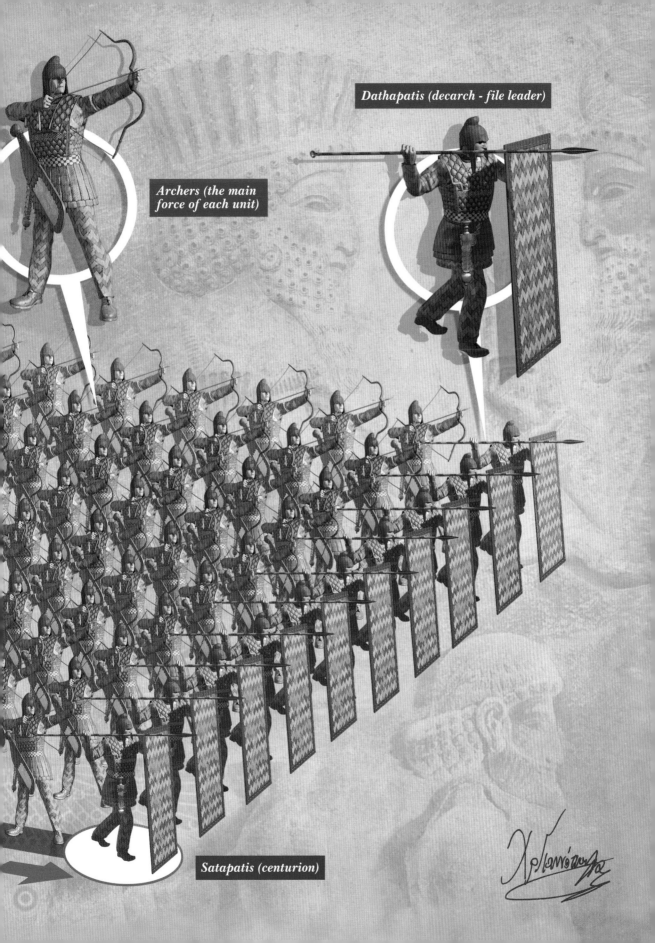

Archers (the main force of each unit)

Dathapatis (decarch - file leader)

Satapatis (centurion)

Charadrus river and waited, drawn up in tactical order, for the Athenian reaction. However, the cautious Athenians, who were without cavalry or archers, were reluctant to begin the battle. They still hoped that the Spartan contingent would arrive in time. In three or four days, the moon would wax full and the Spartan expeditionary force would begin its march to their aid. The Persians, after a nervous wait of many hours, dissolved their formation and returned to their encampment. After all, Datis and Artaphernes had not dared to launch a frontal attack against the strong Greek position.

The Persian challenge, however, caused arguments in the Greek camp. According to Herodotus, five Athenian generals said they should not go into battle before the arrival of the Spartans. Despite this, Miltiades was obstinate and, together with the other four generals, maintained that they should attack only at the proper time. Callimachus agreed with this and, thus, it was decided to launch an attack at the first suitable moment.

It is also possible that, during this time, Hippias may have contacted his supporters and asked them to surrender the city. When all was ready, the conspirators would flash a signal from Mt. Pendeli using a polished shield against the sun. However, there are no reliable sources as to what such a signal would imply. It can only be supposed that it meant the conspirators were ready to open the gates of Athens. The Persians would then send part of their fleet, carrying a strike force, including a contingent of cavalry, round Cape Sounion and attempt a landing at Phaleron. While this was happening, the Athenian hoplites would have to remain where they were at Marathon because of the proximity of the main Persian force. As soon as Athens fell, the Persian force would march on to Marathon via the same road the Athenians had taken and cut off their sole avenue of retreat. Thus, the Athenians would be forced to fight on two fronts.

The Persian generals must have known the reasons for the delay of the Spartan contingent. However, from the moment the moon waxed full, any further delay in the region would be very dangerous. It seems logical to assume that the Persians waited in trepidation for the signal from Mt. Pendeli.

Treason – or in this case, the national solidarity of the Greeks – struck at the Persian camp. A short time before dawn on the day of the battle, a number of Ionian scouts serving in the Persian army slipped out under cover of darkness and arrived at the Athenian wall of wooden obstacles to relay the message that has since become proverbial: "Without horsemen"–(«χωρίς ιππείς».) It was true! The Persian cavalry had moved off the plain. The relevant information concerning this event comes from the Greek historian Ephorus (fourth century B.C.), the Roman historian, Cornelius Nepos, and the 10th century A.D. lexicographer Suidas. The latter's entry, explaining the absence of cavalry from the area states, "When Datis had invaded Attica, they say that the Ionians, after his withdrawal, climbed trees and signaled to the Athenians that the cavalry were away." It is, therefore, possible that, during the night, Datis had taken the cavalry and sailed secretly for Phaleron Bay. Although Herodotus does not confirm this and, despite the fact that such an action would have been contrary to established Persian tactics that dictated close cooperation between cavalry and infantry, such an

explanation does appear plausible. N.G.L. Hammond has another, equally plausible view in which the cavalry was temporarily transferred to the Persian camp for the night, when control of horses in the open plain would be very difficult. Hammond's view is that the Persians were surprised by the Athenian challenge to battle and had no time to deploy their cavalry. When the two armies stood facing each other, the horsemen took up a position behind the infantry, as they required more time to prepare, resulting in their inability to offer substantial assistance. That said, this view is not confirmed by any other source. In addition, the level of training of the Persian infantry must not be underestimated. The foot soldiers could open their line at will at given points to permit the cavalry to pass through to the front. Also, as the horses were withdrawn from the plain each evening, why had the Athenians not started the battle on any of the previous days?

Whatever the explanation, the news of the absence of cavalry was very pleasing to Miltiades' ears. The experienced general realized he now had a unique opportunity to literally grab victory. The news must have also caused a modicum of unease. If, indeed, a sizeable force under Datis was on its way to Phaleron to invest Athens, the time factor was now extremely crucial. Even with a favoring wind, Datis could not reach Phaleron in less than nine to 10 hours, and it would then take around 12 hours to disembark his force. Arthaphernes, for his part, was now left with just the archers and a smaller force. If the Athenians managed to draw him into battle and defeat him, they might have enough time to return to Athens and face Datis. To be sure, the hoplites would be tired from the battle, and it would be hard to cover the 42-kilometer distance from Marathon to Athens in less than seven or eight hours. The outcome could depend on a time span of just a few minutes. The Athenians would have to move at maximum speed. Callimachus agreed with Miltiades and decided to risk such an engagement.

There is no doubt that Miltiades must have formed a plan of action in the preceding days, which he now presented to his fellow generals. They accepted it. But, what was this plan that would give the Athenian phalanx

A Roman sarcophagus cover that is considered to depict the battle around the ships at Marathon. On the left, a Persian warrior is biting an Athenian hoplite on the leg, while an Athenian drags another Persian off his horse. In the center, Aeschylus is holding his dying brother Cynaigeiros and protecting him with his shield from a Persian's ax. On the right, a few Persians attempt to board their vessels. (Archeological Museum of Breschia)

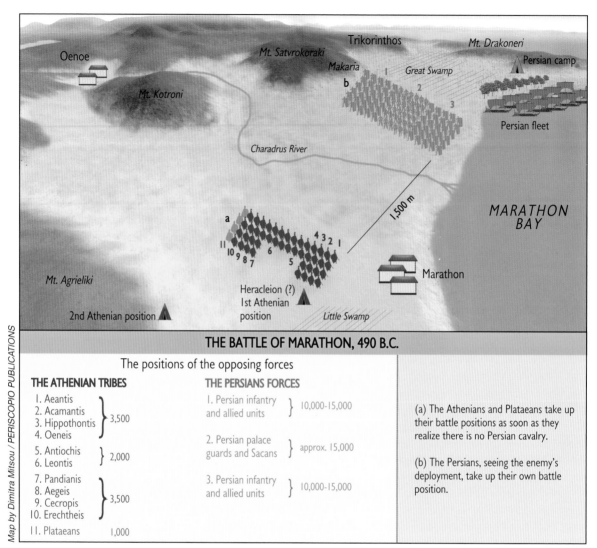

Map by Dimitra Mitsou / PERISCOPIO PUBLICATIONS

THE BATTLE OF MARATHON, 490 B.C.

The positions of the opposing forces

THE ATHENIAN TRIBES		THE PERSIANS FORCES	
1. Aeantis 2. Acamantis 3. Hippothontis 4. Oeneis	} 3,500	1. Persian infantry and allied units }	10,000-15,000
5. Antiochis 6. Leontis	} 2,000	2. Persian palace guards and Sacans }	approx. 15,000
7. Pandianis 8. Aegeis 9. Cecropis 10. Erechtheis	} 3,500	3. Persian infantry and allied units }	10,000-15,000
11. Plataeans	1,000		

(a) The Athenians and Plataeans take up their battle positions as soon as they realize there is no Persian cavalry.

(b) The Persians, seeing the enemy's deployment, take up their own battle position.

the chance to offset the numerical superiority of the enemy and defeat them? Miltiades, without altering the traditional parallel battle formation, included, for the first time on a field of battle, the innovation of tactical surprise.

Everything hinged on Miltiades' knowledge of the opponent. Each of the Great King's armies included Persian and "allied" units from the occupied countries. The Persians and Medes were the army's elite battalions and were prepared to fight to the death. In contrast, the battalions from the subjugated countries did not possess the same fighting efficiency.

For this reason, the Persian commanders placed the allied units on the army's flanks. So, even if these weaker units succumbed to enemy pressure, the elite Persian units in the center would continue the battle. The Persian armies usually consisted of a huge number of troops and the collapse of one, or even two wings would not result in them being outflanked, as the front line was very extended. This fact alone made an outflanking maneuver almost impossible. However, at Marathon, the Persian army did not consist of a huge number of troops, which meant that, if the two flanks were decimated, it

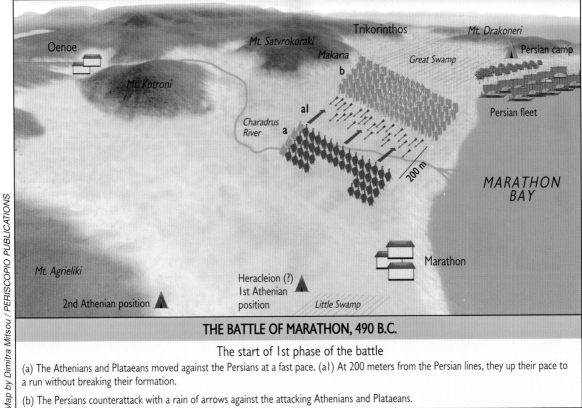

THE BATTLE OF MARATHON, 490 B.C.

The start of 1st phase of the battle

(a) The Athenians and Plataeans moved against the Persians at a fast pace. (a1) At 200 meters from the Persian lines, they up their pace to a run without breaking their formation.

(b) The Persians counterattack with a rain of arrows against the attacking Athenians and Plataeans.

Map by Dimitra Mitsou / PERISCOPIO PUBLICATIONS

would face serious problems.

The Persians took up a position between Mt. Stavrokoraki and the sea. The mountain protected their right flank, while the left flank was protected by the shoreline. To the rear of their army was the Great Swamp, a fact that could lead to total destruction in the event of retreat. So, if both flanks could be destroyed simultaneously, the situation would become untenable for the elite warriors of the center as they could then be attacked from the sides and rear and slain.

Militades had reached this conclusion and so his compatriots had to present an opposite battle formation to that of the Persians, namely strong flanks and a comparatively weak center. The plan of a double outflanking maneuver was behind this battle formation. The Athenian general envisaged that the Persian center would advance at the moment the forces on their flanks retreated under pressure from his own reinforced flanks. The Persian center would, thus, find itself surrounded at the very moment it believed it had beaten its opponent. There is no doubt that such a maneuver required precise movement by the phalanx, but the hoplites' constant, intensive training was a guarantee that they could execute it well and with the required precision.

The battle

It was 5:30 a.m., and the Athenians had taken up their battle positions. Seeing them, the Persians did likewise, seemingly somewhat surprised, as their opponent's inactivity over the past few days had persuaded them that the Greeks were not ready to do battle. The Greek phalanx took up a position between Mt. Kotroni and the sea, with the following composition: On the right, and honorary wing, stood the tribes of Aeantis, Acamantis, Hippothontis and Oeneis, in an eight-man deep formation (simple phalanx) and covering a front of 500 meters (125 meters for each tribe), commanded by Callimachus, as "at that time it was ruled that the polemarch led the right wing." (Herodotus, 6, 111) The Antiochis and Leontis tribes, co-commanded by Themistocles and Aristides, took up the center position in a four-man-deep formation (half-phalanx) across an extended front also of 500 meters. The Pandionis, Aegeis, Kekropis, Erectheis tribes and including the Plataeans, comprised the left wing in an eight-man deep formation, covering a front of 625 meters. The total battle frontage was 1,625 meters, which was identical to the Persian front. While there exists little exact information concerning the Persian battle line, it is known that the palace guards and the Sacans were positioned in the center. These were the elite troops from the Persian Empire's eastern frontiers. The less battle-worthy units were probably positioned on the wings. The Persian formation must have had the same depth across its whole frontage - namely 40-50 men deep.

The Persian battle plan was, perhaps, the opposite to that of the Greeks. The archers would attempt to decimate the enemy phalanx with a rain of arrows, and then the elite units of the Persian center would overrun the enemy's center. In a final phase, the Persian center would first surround one of the wings and then repeat the maneuver with the other, if these had not already retreated following the collapse of the center and under pressure from the Persian wings.

The distance between each hoplite was one meter, and their 90-centimeter diameter shields were hung on their left arms. The shields protected the right side of the man on the left, and they were very close to each other.

The Persians formations were, on the other hand, not so tightly packed as those of the Athenians so as to enable the archers to fire their bows more easily. So, instead of the one meter between the Athenians, it is calculated that each Persian occupied a frontal width of 1.4 meters, giving a frontline of, at least, 1,100 men. Then, if it is assumed that the battle formation was 40 or 50 men deep, the total number of Persian warriors rises to between 44,000 and 55,000. It could well be that the Persian force was smaller than this, if it is also assumed that Datis was on his way to Athens with a significant number of the expeditionary force.

Was there an inherent weakness in Miltiades' plan or something else that could overturn the Athenian expectations, leading to a total defeat? Modern military analysts and historians agree that there was a grave danger of the Athenian center collapsing. This could occur, as Miltiades had expanded the width of the phalanx to avoid encirclement, while, simultaneously, also reinforcing his wings resulting in the center units lacking depth so, in that sense, weakening them. Therefore, it was crucially important that the two tribes holding the center were able to withstand the assault of the elite Persian infantry until the Athenian wings had managed to repulse their opposing enemy formations. However, the Athenians held a number of other advantages over their opponents that guaranteed the survival of their center. The discipline, tactics, weapons, and protective armor of the Athenians were much superior to those of the Persians. In particular, the Greek hoplite's weapons were incomparably superior to those of any other warrior's weapons in existence anywhere at that time. At Marathon, it was the battle of the long spear versus the short javelin, the long sword versus the short sword, the metal breast armor versus padded linen breast protection, the bronze-lined shields versus wooden ones, and, finally, Greek metal helmets versus the Phrygian helmets.

The Athenians took up their battle positions and began their traditional sacrifices that, once again, brought favorable omens for the battle's outcome - "the slaughtered meats were favorable" writes Herodotus (6, 112). Immediately after the sacrificial rites the signal was given to attack. The bronze-clad army of 10,000 men moved as one, fast and completely silent. The distance separating the two armies was about 1,500 meters (eight furlongs, according to Herodotus). Therefore, the view of the Greek historian that the Athenians and Plataeans ran the whole distance does not appear to be correct. If the 32 kilograms of weaponry each man carried is taken into consideration, along with the season's high temperatures, although it was still early morning, and the three-hour battle that ensued, it must be concluded that the hoplites would have been exhausted, if not before the end of the battle, then surely during their return to Athens. In addition, they were expected to fall on the enemy with great force and inertia and this certainly could not have been achieved if they had already run a distance of 1,500 meters. It is reasonable, then, to suppose that they approached the enemy at a fast pace,

without singing martial paeons, otherwise they would have run out of breath. What is more, if they had run the whole distance, there would be a high risk of losing the coherence and synchronization of their phalanx.

The range of the Persian bows was around 200 meters. At a shorter distance of between 100 and 150 meters, the Persian archers were precise, deadly marksmen. Thus, the Athenians and Plataeans upped their rapid pace to a fast run only during the final 200 meters in order to avoid, as much as possible, losses from the dense rain of arrows.

The Persians stood stunned as they viewed the amazing spectacle of the

The bust of Aeschylus. The prominent Athenian considered that the glory of his participation in the "Marathon grove" battle could neither be compared with his artistic creations nor with the glory of the naval battles of Artemisium and Salamis. (Rome, Istituto Archeologico Germaniko)

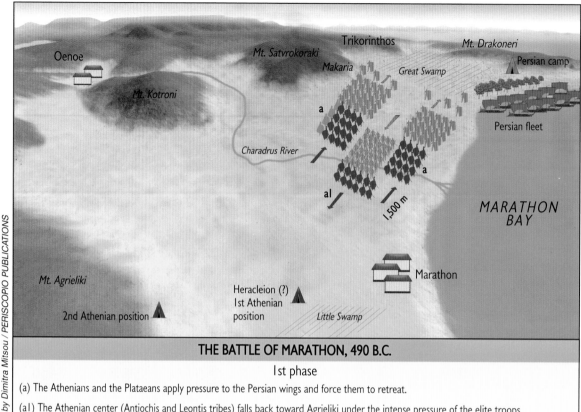

Map by Dimitra Mitsou / PERISCOPIO PUBLICATIONS

THE BATTLE OF MARATHON, 490 B.C.

1st phase

(a) The Athenians and the Plataeans apply pressure to the Persian wings and force them to retreat.

(a1) The Athenian center (Antiochis and Leontis tribes) falls back toward Agrieliki under the intense pressure of the elite troops of the Persian center.

advancing hoplite assault. Without doubt, they thought the Athenians must have taken leave of their senses to attack in this manner, without cavalry or archer support, and it would lead them, with mathematical accuracy, to their death: "And in their minds they charged the Athenians with madness which must be fatal, seeing that they were few and yet were pressing forward at a run, having neither cavalry nor archers. Such was the thought of the Barbarians" (Herodotus, 6, 112). As soon as the Athenians came into range, the Persian archers launched a hailstorm of arrows, but the Athenians' speed and their heavy defensive armor allowed them to pass through it almost unscathed. During the ensuing moments, the dumbstruck Persians in the first ranks saw the aimed spears of the Athenian phalanx. For most of

them, it was the last thing they were to see on this earth. The hoplites fell on the Persian ranks in great strength. The terrible sound of the clashing shields signaled the start of the battle. The first three ranks of the phalanx advanced with spears extended horizontally and drove them into the Persian bodies. The remaining ranks pushed from behind with great force. The forward thrust of the hoplites was tremendous as, by pushing with their left shoulder against their shields, they exerted great pressure on the men in front. The inertia of the clash and the initial pressure resulted in the crushing of the first ranks of the Persians. After the initial Persian surprise, the battle continued in earnest along the whole front line. The right-wing hoplites, commanded by the polemarch, Callimachus, were particularly successful, striking the

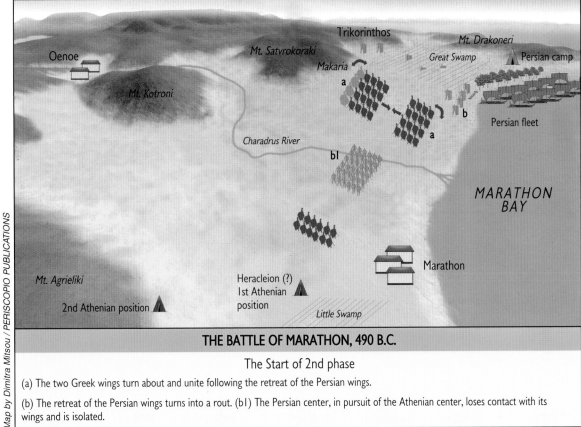

THE BATTLE OF MARATHON, 490 B.C.

The Start of 2nd phase

(a) The two Greek wings turn about and unite following the retreat of the Persian wings.

(b) The retreat of the Persian wings turns into a rout. (b1) The Persian center, in pursuit of the Athenian center, loses contact with its wings and is isolated.

enemy especially hard. The left wing soon experienced the same success: "On both wings the Athenians and Plataeans were winning the victory; and they left that part of the Barbarians which had been routed to flee without molestation" (Herodotus, 6, 113).

The Athenians succeeded in overrunning the first ranks of the wings, with the result that they could then turn round and attack the Persians from the rear This was followed by the collapse of the battalions of both wings throughout the whole of their depth, forcing the Persians into a desperate flight toward the sea.

Meanwhile, the opposite was occurring in the center, where "the barbarians were winning" (Herodotus, 6, 113). A this point, the two Athenian tribes, with Aristides and Themistocles fighting in the first line as mere hoplites, were under extraordinary pressure and began an orderly retreat according to the preconceived plan. The Persian center pursued them, causing a few casualties on the way. Despite all this pressure, they managed to successfully complete their mission by keeping the elite enemy units engaged throughout the whole time it took for the two Greek wings to achieve victory on both flanks. Even though they were retreating, the hoplites continued to keep the Persians busy. This rearward movement by the Athenian center was, by all accounts, executed with exemplary unity even though it had been weakened due to the unavoidable increase in the distance between the center and the two wings that were, throughout this time, executing their opposite offensive maneuver.

The battle's first phase ended with a speedy Athenian victory on both wings and a retreat in the center. During the actual fighting, there had been a satisfactory time delay and adequate resistance by the Athenian center to achieve the planned objectives of Miltiades. The two Persian wings had been put out of action and were no longer able to play any decisive role in the battle. The size of the Persian force had been reduced to less than half its initial strength, and its center units had been isolated. In contrast, the Athenian and Plataean wings remained intact and battle-ready and were, therefore, available to continue the battle.

The time factor also proved to be very crucial during the battle's second phase. The two wings had to unite before the still strong enemy center had a chance turn around and attack. At this critical juncture, Greek discipline and training proved its worth. According to experts in the art of war, few things are more difficult to control than retreat and pursuit. However, the Athenians and Plataeans were able to disengage according to the plan. As soon as the Athenians and Plataeans succeeded in overrunning the enemy sections facing them, forcing them to flee, they avoided pursuing them although, admittedly, it was quite tempting to do so. Any pursuit would have resulted in the sacrifice of the still hard-fighting center. So, they maintained their discipline, keeping a distance of 500 to 600 meters between them. According to the plan and, as disciplined as ever, they about-faced and joined into one solid phalanx. To gain an insight into the amazingly high level of training and discipline in the Athenian hoplite ranks, all these maneuvers were carried out in less than two minutes. A very large, eight-man deep phalanx,

totaling 8,000 men, was now ready to attack the Persian center from the rear. The newly formed phalanx was a reversal of the initial formation; in other words, on the left side now stood the Athenians commanded by Callimachus, while on the right stood the Plataeans. This time, the men in the front ranks were those who had been in the rear ranks of the previous formation ("the tail-draggers"). This change did not, in the slightest, diminish the fighting strength of the phalanx, as the rear rank men were always, and by standard practice, experienced warriors for just this type of maneuver. The Athenian phalanx, with a frontage of 1,100 meters, now advanced without delay toward the enemy rear and, in under two minutes, fell upon them. The distance between the two armies was no greater than 500 meters, and the battle that ensued was stubbornly fought and very deadly. The men of the Persian center, encouraged by the retreat of the corresponding Athenian center, fought tenaciously and with bravery equaling that of their opponents, justifying their elite warrior status. They were the finest Persian warriors and were excellently trained and very well armed. Despite the decimation of their wings, they still retained a small numerical superiority of about 15,000 men. However, the sight that met them as they turned around to meet the bold charge of the hoplites in their rear - which may have forced them to hurriedly extend their front - allied to the counterattack attack of the quickly reforming Athenian center, brought victory to the Greeks.

On the Greek right wing, the fighting Plataeans probably clashed with an enemy unit of excellent fighting ability, which they were unable to overcome. However, on the left wing, where Callimachus was, and along the rest of the line "the Athenians finally won." (Herodotus, 6,113) Despite the Persians' desperate resistance, the courage and power of the Athenian charge proved irresistible. The Persian forces on the right flank and in the center collapsed. In a desperate effort to save themselves, they crashed into their own left flank, causing all to flee toward the beach of Schinias. This was the end of the battle's second phase, which saw the elite forces of the Persian expeditionary force broken and routed.

The battle around the ships

Although the second phase of Miltiades' plan had succeeded, those enemy forces that had managed to withdraw to the ships remained dangerous and could start new offensive operations. For this reason, the Athenians and Plataeans set about a relentless pursuit of the beaten foe. Many of the fleeing Persians became lost in the general confusion that reigned and blundered into the Great Swamp, suffering heavy losses. Their pitiless pursuers immediately killed those lucky enough to be able to be reached, but many others suffered an agonizingly slow death as they sank into the depth of the swamp. However, the majority of the Persians managed to retreat to the narrow strip between the Great Swamp and the sea, the beach of Schinias, in order to board their ships. The Athenians closely pursued them, and it was here that the battle's fiercest, most desperate fighting took place, as the Persians sought to hurriedly board their ships while the Athenians tried to set fire to the enemy vessels to prevent them from escaping. The Athenian generals sought the total destruction

of the invaders so they would not have to face a new offensive against their city in the future. Many modern authors put forward the premise that if, at this stage, the Persians had somehow managed to reform, then the whole balance of the opposing forces would have changed spectacularly. This was because, at that moment, the battle was not being fought by the close-knit, solid body of the hoplite phalanx, but had developed into isolated individual man-to-man duels.

When battles are fought "on paper" all possibilities remain open. However, theory is a far cry from action. It would have been impossible for the panicked Persians to reform and counterattack in a few minutes. Even if they had managed to reform, it is also certain that the Greek hoplites

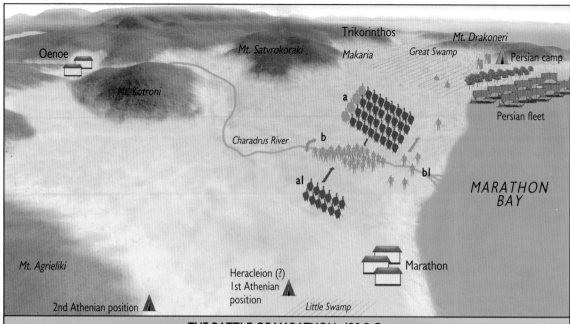

THE BATTLE OF MARATHON, 490 B.C.

2nd phase

(a) The two Greek wings, making a fast turn-about and uniting into one phalanx, attack the Persian center.

(a1) The Athenian center counter-attacks.

(b) The Persian center tries to turn around in order to face the phalanx, attacking it from the rear.

(b1) The units of the Persian center break up their formation and retreat in disorder toward the ships while many men drown in the nearby Great Swamp.

would have instantly transformed themselves into a murderous metal mass or, failing that, into smaller organized attacking groups as the pine-filled ground of Schinias would not allow for the full deployment of a military force.

In addition, the battle around the ships concerned just the last ranks of the Persian center as, in the meantime, the wings and front ranks (formerly the rear ranks before being attacked from the rear) of the center had already boarded their ships and were sailing away. The fighting was extremely desperate, as the Persians fought for their lives, while the Athenians, as if under the spell of some "Dionysiac trance," attempted to massacre every last enemy warrior. Many prominent Persians were killed, while the Athenians lost Callimachus and General Stesilaus. A special,

almost mythical place in history has been reserved for the struggle by Cynaegeirus, the son of Euphorion (the brother of the tragic poet Aeschylus, who also fought at Marathon). As he attempted to stop a ship from sailing by holding it by the stern, a Persian ax cut off both his arms, and he died as a result. Other prominent Athenians also met their death here. What is disturbing is that from the moment victory had been achieved, they could have saved themselves if they had remained aloof from the relentless pursuit. But, this was in an era when the nobles upheld their honor and titles by fighting in the frontline, and not by hanging the family shields on the castle walls and telling tales about the heroic deeds of his ancestors.

It was 8:30 a.m. before the Persians finally managed to sail away after

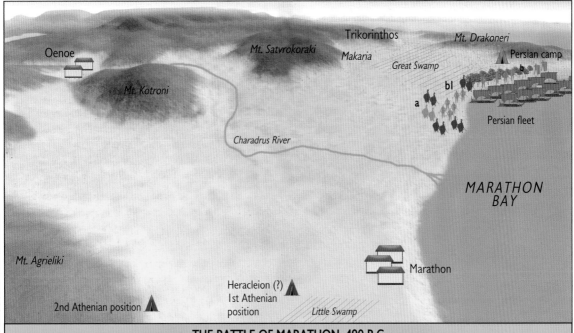

Map by Dimitra Mitsou / PERISCOPIO PUBLICATIONS

THE BATTLE OF MARATHON, 490 B.C.

The battle around the ships

(a) The Athenians and the Plataeans break out from their formation and relentlessly pursue the Persians.

(b) Most of the Persian units (those of the two wings and the first ones of the center) have already boarded the ships.

(b1) The last Persian units of the center do not board the ships in time and are slain by the Athenians and the Plataeans.

losing seven ships and with the victory cries of the Athenians and Plataeans ringing loud in their ears. The plain of Marathon lay strewn with the 6,400 corpses of the slain invaders. Among them also lay 192 Athenians, whose blood had been shed for the freedom of their city.

It had been a glorious victory that had been won due to the bravery and self-sacrifice of the Athenians and Plataeans, Miltiades ingenious plan, and the training and weapons of the Greek warriors.

The race

While the defeat was a serious setback for the invaders, it was not a total disaster. The Persian army still possessed intact almost the whole of its fleet and all of its cavalry force. The majority of its infantry remained battle-worthy, although its morale had been dealt a serious blow by the unexpected defeat. According to Herodotus, the Persian vessels sailed from Marathon, stopped on the island Aegilia to take aboard some Eretrian prisoners they had previously left, and headed toward Cape Sounion. Artaphernes still intended to reach Phaleron Bay, land his forces and move against Athens before the Athenians had time to return from Marathon. The Greek historian states that the conspirators' infamous signal was given, informing the Persians that the city was poorly defended: "and an accusation became current among the Athenians to the effect that they formed this design by contrivance of the Alcmaionidai; for these, it was said, having concerted matters with the Persians, displayed to them a shield when they had now embarked in their ships" (Herodotus, 6, 115).

However, the voyage to Phaleron took some considerable time. Their sojourn at Aegilia had shown they were in no great haste. The most possible explanation is that Datis had sailed away during the night and headed for Phaleron, and now the remainder of the fleet was on its way to reinforce him. So, if what they had already achieved was not enough, the Athenians now had to rush to save their city. Aristides and his hoplites from the Antiochis tribe had remained behind on the Marathon battlefield to guard the rich spoils and the wounded, while Miltiades, with the nine other tribes, was rushing to arrive in Athens by the Kifissia road before a Persian landing took place. Even today it seems admirable that the Athenians were willing to embark on this coordinated march without complaint and that they managed to drag their feet that distance after three hours of battle. But, the impetus behind their sacrifice was that their families waited and they had to save them. Although exhausted, they expended almost all their remaining energy on this unbelievable race against time. "The Athenians ran to their city as fast as they could." They arrived in time, around 4:30 p.m. - 5 p.m., and bivouacked by the temple of Heracles at Cynosarges - "they started from the temple of Heracles at Marathon and arrived at another temple of Heracles at Cynosarges." At sunset, the Persian fleet appeared in Phaleron Bay. Although it is not known whether they waited to see a sun signal from a shield raised aloft by a traitor, but what they saw instead must have shocked them and removed all thoughts of disembarking. Instead of a single signal, the rays of the setting sun reflected on 8,000 shields that sent out a clear message that, as long as Athens

could count on warriors such as these, it would be impossible to conquer it. The Persians lingered awhile with sails set and then painfully "started again on their way back to Asia" (Herodotus, 6, 116).

So, the Battle of Marathon had reached its conclusion. The Persians had departed for the time being, but they were destined to return 10 years later. The aged Hippias had missed his final chance of reinstating the dynasty of the Peisistratides. He was soon to die a disappointed man during his return journey to Sigeion. The conspirators must have been equally disappointed. P. Green writes that "many must have been the people in Athens who changed sides silently and hastily."

Three days after the battle, as Herodotus writes, the 2,000 Spartan hoplites arrived in Athens. "After the full moon the Lacedaemonians sent 2,000 warriors to Athens who arrived very quickly as they covered the distance from Sparta to Attica in three days" (Herodotus, 6, 120). Plato (Menexenus, 240d) and Isocrates both state that the Spartans arrived on the day after the battle, covering a distance of 1,200 furlongs (240 kilometers) in three days. As soon they were informed of the battle's outcome, they asked to see the dead Persians. In fact, they went to Marathon and, after congratulating the Athenians, departed for their homeland, with the possible thought that a new rival power was on the rise in Greece.

The Athenians buried their dead on the battlefield with great honors. It was the first time that dead defenders of the city had not been buried in the Kerameikos cemetery of Athens but, instead, were laid to rest in a special common grave, the Tymbus or Soros. Pausanias mentions another tomb for the Plataeans and the slaves, despite the fact that it is very doubtful that slaves had taken part in the battle, even as auxiliaries. There is, however, no chance that the Athenians' faithful allies were not buried separately. Professor Spyros Marinatos believes that there were two separate tombs, one for the Plataeans and one for the slaves. Pausanias of Sparta states that the Athenians buried the Persians as custom dictated and as befitting the dead, and as claimed by the Athenians themselves. But, he adds, he was unable to discover even one grave and so supposes they were thrown into a large ditch. Their number must have been too great to bury them all with the usual formalities. The Spartan traveler also offers an interesting piece of information. He states that when Miltiades died he was buried at Marathon.

Significance and review of the battle

The Greek victory at Marathon was an event of enormous military and political significance. Some modern historians claim that the battle was not decisive, as the Persians returned ten years later. They have not, however, given thought to the fact that, even if the Persians initially limited themselves to a submission and destruction of the city, no one would have been able to prevent them from launching an even greater campaign for the conquest of all of Greece at a later date. The only formidable power able to stop them would have been Sparta, but it is doubtful if Sparta would have been able to stop the Persian storm unaided and alone.

The view that the Persian invasion was a limited campaign that set out merely to punish Eretria and Athens cannot be proven by historical analysis. The Persian invasion was the prelude to the larger effort of Persia's expansion in the West. The most significant evidence of this is the fact that Xerxes' campaign of 480-479 B.C. was carried out with a military force unequaled in size in world history till then, and remaining so for hundreds of years after.

Persia was a mighty empire, stretching from India to the Aegean Sea and from the Black Sea to Egypt. Mainland Greece was, on the one hand, the entry point for the possible Persian expansion into Europe while, on the other hand, it controlled a sizeable proportion of the known world's sea trade. The Scythian campaign is indicative of the Persian's expansion plan. With the Ionian coast, Thrace, and Macedonia conquered, central and southern Greece was, obviously, the Persian's next likely goal. It was this goal that the Athenians and Plataeans of Marathon had negated, temporarily perhaps, but giving the Greeks 10 years' grace to see the danger and prepare for the next decisive struggle.

A Corinthian-style helmet is inscribed with the words «Μιλτιάδης ανέθεκεν τω Διί»– "Miltiades offered it to Zeus." It was discovered in Zeus' temple at Olympia and, according to one view, is a votive offering of Miltiades after his victory at the Battle of Marathon. Another view claims that the helmet is from approximately 520 B.C. because of its shape and the type of alphabet used. In this case, it may have been offered by an Athenian general to celebrate a later military engagement at Marathon. (Archeological Museum of Olympia)

The painting of the famous crater vase by the "painter of Darius," titled "Persians." In the center, Darius presides over his Empire Council. The bearded man standing in front of him is a messenger who is obviously announcing the news of the Persian defeat at Marathon. (Naples, National Museum)

The moral benefits of the Battle of Marathon were significant. The warriors of Marathon destroyed the myth of Persian invincibility, opening the way for the great triumphs of Salamis and Plataea.

On the Persian side, defeat at the Battle of Marathon imposed some hard lessons. The Persian losses were insignificant when compared to the huge expanse and human capacity of the Persian Empire. The next attempt would be made on a much larger scale, with better organization and infinitely greater forces and means.

The Battle of Marathon also proved the superiority of Greek weapons and tactics. First, it proved the survivability of the phalanx under a heavy onslaught by archers – under conditions that other, very powerful armies, including the Lydians, Carians, Babylonians, Assyrians, Egyptians etc., had succumbed. The arrows had proven inadequate when faced with a tightly packed phalanx. At Marathon, the hoplites attacked the Persian archers at an ever-growing pace while the arrows used against them were unable to penetrate the Grecian shields. As seen, the Athenians had to cover a distance of 1,500 meters before coming into contact with the Persian lines. During the final 200 meters, they had upped their pace to a run and passed through the falling wall of Persian arrows. In fact, they had found themselves within range of the Persian archers for less than 40 seconds, and in that time they had suffered one minor casualty. Many contemporary researchers say that it was impossible for such heavily armed men, under such high temperatures, to cover that distance at a run without dropping from exhaustion. However, what they neglect to explain is how these same warriors were able to fight for three hours after that, as, according to them, they had proved unable to run for 200 meters. Even today, traversing an area under observation or under fire is made with the whole force united and at a run.

Athenian hoplite, 490 B.C.
The young Athenian hoplite shown here is wearing cheap armor of painted leather on the upper part of his body, a painted Corinthian crestless helmet and painted greaves. His shield features one of the characteristic swastika-like emblems of the democratic faction of the Alcmaeonids, the "tetraskelion" or "tetraskelon," surrounded by the red ring that shows the old relationship of the faction to the Delphi Oracle. The reddish paint of the greaves and the helmet functions as a mean of personal recognition mark within the file and rank of the phalanx and protects the metal from gradual oxidization.
(uniform research and reconstruction-illustration: Christos Giannopoulos)

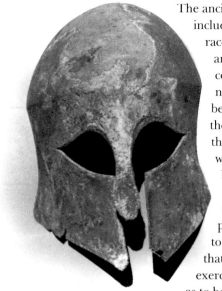

A Corinthian style helmet. (Cyprus, Museum of Nicosia)

The ancient Greeks had not included the running race in their Olympics and in other competitions for nothing. It must also be remembered that the bodily fitness of the men of that era was clearly much better than our own today. A look at the statues from the period is sufficient to make us realize that the ancient Greeks exercised intensively so as to be able to meet the needs of man-to-man battle, where the winner was always the one who was physically fitter and better trained and who had also been indoctrinated with the idea that there is no greater shame in battle than abandoning the warrior next to you. Finally, the emotional charge of the moment must not be forgotten – a factor adding enormous strength to the Athenian warriors. The hoplites were the final barrier between the invaders and their families, properties and the graves of their ancestors. Their awareness of what was at stake, combined with the fighting spirit found in all real warriors, unleashed tremendous physical and psychological powers. As Hanson correctly points out, "the hoplite of the phalanx had to concentrate all his bravery into an uninhibited frenzy of activity. For one or two hours he had to stretch himself beyond the limits of his physical and psychological endurance" (Hanson 2003, 57). The Athenians then went through the barrier of arrows and fell like an avalanche of snow on the Persians. The speed they had attained made the clash even more effective. During the aftermath, events followed the course

Miltiades had predicted, and the Athenians won the battle and saved not only Athens but all of western European civilization as well. As Fuller writes, "Marathon was the first birth-cry of the Europe that was getting born."

The Marathon victory gave eternal glory and fame to Militiades, the man who had conceived its strategic and tactical plan. One of the elements that gave Miltiades' tactics greater value was synchronization. By that term, we mean the combination of battleground activities in time, space, and objective in such a manner as to achieve superiority at the decisive moment. Hans Delbrück, in his monumental work "Warfare in Antiquity," gives us perhaps the most truthful picture of the battle: "The picture of Miltiades looms large in the early years of international military history. The most complete and rarest form of leadership in battle that was created until today, the combination of defense and offense exists here, within the simple lines of the classic work of art of the first great military event in our history. What foresight in the choice of battleground, what self-control while waiting for the enemy attack, what discipline of the masses, in the army of the proud, democratic citizens, so that he could hold them at the position he had chosen and then lead them to attack at the crucial moment! All had been arranged to lead to this moment: not a minute less and not a minute more, as then the Athenians would arrive breathless before the enemy and, by then, many of the enemy arrows would have found their target and the man that fell or hesitated would delay and stop the advance of the charge that had to fall like an avalanche on the opponent in order to obtain victory. In the future we shall have occasion to analyze such similar cases, but never one that is greater."

The battle of Marathon, apart from destroying the myth of Persian invincibility, aside from the boost to the fighting morale of the Greeks so they could face Xerxes' later invasion, drove men such as Xenophon and Agesilaus to lead their warriors to war in Asia and to reveal to Alexander the military weaknesses of the Persians.

If the history of warfare is studied further, it can be seen that Miltiades' ingenious maneuver at Marathon was repeated on a scale that befitted each particular method of fighting, each specific battle, at each moment in later times. Darius III, the Codomanus, tried unsuccessfully to apply the same principle against Alexander at Gaugamela. Hannibal applied it with complete success at the Battle of Cannae (A.D. 216). More recently, Blücher used it at Waterloo, Moltke at Sedan, and Hindenburg used it at Tannenberg against the Tsarist army, achieving the greatest victory of World War I. General Eisenhower used it during the battle of France following the Normandy landings. However, those who admitted they had been very attentive during their Greek history lessons were the German generals of World War II. The famous tactic of the "hammer and anvil maneuver" derives from Miltiades. In Poland in 1939, the mechanized wings of the German invaders broke the Polish frontline forces, and a large proportion of the Polish Army was trapped by pincer movements and destroyed. During the invasion of France in 1940, the two attacking German wings had the mission to break through the enemy line and advance as deeply as they were able through the enemy formation and then encircle and destroy the French forces that lay between the two

breakthrough points they had opened, just like the Athenian wings had done after they had neutralized the corresponding Persian forces at Marathon when they encircled the Persian center with the help of their own center and destroyed it. The same tactic was followed during the invasion of the Soviet Union in 1941. Three battles of the Marathon type were all that was needed for the German divisions to arrive before the gates of Moscow. The German victories were so spectacular and the Soviet Army losses in men and materials so great, that they led Stalin to the verge of panic.

The king of Persia, Darius I. (Relief sculpture from the Palace of Apadana in Persepolis)

However, further than the contribution of the battle of Marathon to world military history, the Athenians and Plataeans had safeguarded the cultural treasures of Athens, and as Sir Edward Shepherd Creasy says in his work "The Fifteen Decisive Battles of the World" their other great contribution was to pave the way for "the development of free institutions, the liberal enlightenment of the western world, and the gradual development over a span of many centuries of the principles of European civilization." In the summer of 490 B.C., the torch of destruction was just 42 kilometers from Athens. It would not be just the city that would burn; it would also halt the advance of western civilization. Alan Lloyd, in his book titled "Marathon," offers a vivid image of what was at stake during

*Greek general, 5th Century B.C.
The rank of general denoted the leader,
or commander of an army and was used
in all the democratic city-states of ancient Greece
– Athens, Syracuse, Taras, Argos, etc. There were
10 generals in Athens, one from each tribe, and the
people elected them all every year. Before being given
power, their character, integrity, and behavior had to
be tested. No one could be elected general if he did not
have his own legal children and property. Their duties
included command of the army, the conduct of all military
preparations, and the solving of all problems connected with
military matters. The generals conscripted and classified
soldiers into categories with the aid of their brigadiers. The
state also tasked the generals with the collection of extra taxes
imposed on citizens' properties for the requirements of warfare.
However, their primary duty remained the command of the
army in time of war. The Athenian fleet was also commanded
by generals, and the flagship was named "the general's ship."
The photo shows a 90-millimeter figure model made by the
Italian company of Pegaso Models (product code number
90-029), which consists of 16 parts. It was sculpted by the
talented artist Andrea Jula and painted by Costas Kariotellis.
It was painted in acrylics, while printing inks were used on
the metal parts. The bronze helmet is of the Corinthian
type with a crest of painted horsehair. The breastplate is
made of scales, while, on its lower edge, hang the wing
flaps – leather strips reinforced on the inside with
metal sheet. Under the breast armor, he wears a
mantle reaching to just above the knees. His lower
legs were protected by bronze greaves. His sandals
were made of leather. His sword, in its scabbard,
was quite long and double-edged. The spear
had an overall length of 3 meters with
pointed heads at each end and a shaft of
wood. The shaft shown here is shorter –
denoting that the bearer is an infantry
general. The round shield was made of
bronze and wood and decorated
with various designs –in this case
the mythical griffin. (Photos and
text by Stelios Demiras, Model
Expert magazine)*

Athenian Hoplite Elite unit of the 300 "Logades," 490 B.C.

Though no special mention of participation of an elite corps of hoplites exists, we know that 300 Athenian hoplites were especially selected for their high moral integrity, their excellent physique, and their fighting experience. These were formed into a special assault corps at the beginning of the fifth century B.C. known as the "Logades," a usual practice that existed in almost all of the Greek city-states then. The "Logas" warrior depicted here is wearing rather expensive armor (a combination of successive layers of leather, cloth, lamellar, and metal scale armor) that is adapted to his body and to the needs of movement in man-to-man battle. His "open" Attic helmet, its horse-hair crest, and his cloth-made shoulder straps have been decorated with the typical bi-colored checker pattern that was popular among Athenian hoplites and also among their Persian opponents of the time.

The hoplite's shield bears the face of the Gorgon, the mother of Famine and devastation, an emblem of the Eteoboutades clan. In battle conditions, the intense contrast of black, white and red, in conjunction with the threatening face of the shield, caused psychological havoc in nonexperienced opponents. (uniform research and reconstruction-illustration: Christos Giannopoulos) those critical moments of the battle: "Athens, at the time, was famous for the talented citizens it housed and for those soon to be born. Sophocles was still a child. Sophroniscos, the Athenian citizen who was to become the father of Socrates, was, perhaps, already wedded to the mother of the philosopher, Phaenarete. If Athens had fallen that summer, followed by wholesale slaughter, and with the population deported, the chain reaction that a possible loss of the cultural inheritance would cause is beyond any calculation. Without Socrates, what would Plato be? Would he be one who merely had pride in his ancestors who had survived a Persian victory? And without Plato, what would Aristotle be? The loss of Plato would have been unthinkable for western philosophy. We would no longer have his rightful instinct for a reasonable philosophy of ethics, his spiritual search for a truer appreciation of virtues, his vision for the soul, and his whole metaphysical foundation for his theories which inspired later generations and our contemporary civilization. Even if we assume that not these men but other new men would be born at that time and despite the change of the environment, it is very difficult to neglect the general climate and the amazing progress of social institutions that followed the outcome of the Marathon battle."

This historical battle was also a major landmark for Athenian

The tomb of the Athenians who fell in the Battle of Marathon. (Photo by Nikos Giannopoulos, June 2007)

democracy. The new form of government of the city, democracy, had proven its strength. It had proved that it could produce able military leaders, even after ups and downs, setbacks and recoils, and that it could isolate its internal enemies while inspiring the citizens to fight for their homeland and its values. Still, next to the great anonymity of the hoplites' phalanx, the setting star of the aristocratic era was still producing its last heroes: Callimachus, Stesilaus, and Cynaigerus. Accepting as their sacred duty to protect their city, the Athenian hoplites, noblemen or not, had taken their position on the plain of Marathon, ready to sacrifice themselves for the sake of their military honor. That is why they had not fled to the mountains to save themselves, and they had not shut themselves within the city walls to wait for help from either the Spartans or the gods. That is also why they had not hurried to present the tokens of submission, "earth and water," and that is why Callimachus had fallen: It was a matter of military honor. Military honor, fear of losing their homeland, and the military genius of an inspired leader were the causes that had led the Athenians and their brave Plataean allies to the trophy of victory at Marathon. It was "the trophy of Miltiades that would not let Themistocles sleep" (Plutarch, Themistocles 3, 4). It was the everlasting glory of the Marathon fighters that had made Aeschylus to ask people to remember him not for his great poetical work but for that day when he stood in the phalanx in order to fight for the freedom of his country. Aeschylus is believed to have written this epigram to be engraved on his tomb: "This tomb covers Aeschylus, the Athenian, son of Euphorion. For his renowned valor can speak the sacred Marathonian grove and the Persian with the long hair, who knew it well."

Many detailed studies of the battle of Marathon have been written, and many more will be written in the future. One, however, wonders if there is anything that describes it more accurately than this simple epigram of Simonides of Ceos does: "The Athenians, as the defenders of the Greeks at Marathon, destroyed the power of the golden-clad Medes."

A historical interpretation of the Athenian victory

The victory of the Athenians at Marathon was, in later times, viewed as a successful defense of the freedom of Greece from Persian despotism and as proof of the health of the new democratic government of Athens. In reality, however, it was the result of the superior homogeneous Greek culture over the multinational culture of the East.

The battle of Marathon was not merely a military confrontation of two opponents, but rather a decisive battle between two distinct worlds and civilizations. This battle was not a mere clash of the Persian vanguard or a punitive expedition with specific targets, as some historians claim. On the contrary, the expedition to Attica was part of the long-term plan of Persian geopolitics, with the subjugation of Greece and total control of the Aegean Sea as its ultimate goal.

With the expeditionary force, Darius had ordered Datis to be accompanied by Hippias, the tyrant who had been exiled by the Athenians in 510 B.C. His goal was to establish a pro-Persian government that would bring to Greece the weight and influence of the political traditions of Darius' empire and gradually to transform Greece into a territory of the Persian kingdom. Such a regime in the heart of Greece would eventually be able to absorb all the Greek states into the expanding Persian Empire.

Against such a background, the Athenian victory at the Battle of Marathon was a confirmation of the correctness of Cleisthenes' reforms of 509 B.C., when the democratic form of rule was first established. It was not only the aristocracy, but also the lower social classes, the seamen, and the small landowners who had taken part in the battle. The war against the Persian Empire hardened Greeks into a new social unity. War, as the primary revolutionary process throughout history, accelerated the homogeneous growth of the Athenian political body through common sacrifices and common expectations. The various pro-tyrant factions, i.e., the aristocracy and the agricultural classes, gradually came to support the democratic form of rule along with a large percentage of their people. The battle had also proved the value of collective action against the individual action of the aristocratic conception of heroism. And, it was in this way that the rapid development of Athenian democracy started and was later transformed in stages to an imperialistic power within the confines of Greece.

The Ionian column head of the Trophy of the Athenians. (Archeological Museum of Marathon)

The victory of Athenian arms at Marathon has, since ancient times, been seen as a great success of, not only the Athenians but also of the whole of the Greek world. This view is obvious in Simonides' epigram: "The Athenians, as the defenders of the Greeks at Marathon, destroyed the power of the golden-clad Medes." In this epigram, the Athenian hoplites are presented as defenders of all Greeks. The great tragic poet Aeschylus chose to have his tomb inscribed with an epigram that showed his contribution to the battle as the greatest achievement of his life. In the Italian city of Gela, where he was buried, this epigram was inscribed on this tomb: "This tomb covers Aeschylus, the Athenian, son of Euphorion. For his renowned valor can speak the sacred Marathonian grove and the Persian with the long hair, who knew it well."

The Athenians dedicated a tenth of the Persian spoils from the battle to the temple of Apollo at Delphi. These were placed in a small Doric temple known as the "Treasure of the Athenians." As Pausanias adds (Attica, 10, 1), 15 years after the battle, the Athenians put up a large group of bronze statues at the start of the Sacred Way to Delphi, thus connecting their Marathon victory with the defense of Panhellenic values. The battle continued to be honored with special events for a long time by Athenian citizens, while its anniversary was celebrated as late as the first century A.D., as Plutarch states («Πότερον Αθηναίοι..., 349 Ε»).

At a lower social level, a kind of hero-worship appeared later. The

The Treasure House of the Athenians at Delphi. On the small triangular floor in front of the entrance of the little temple is the following inscription: «Αθεναίοι τ[ο]ι Απόλλον[ι από Μέδ]ον ακ[ροθ]'ινια τες Μαραθ[ό]νι μ[άχες]» i.e. "The Athenians offer to Apollo one-tenth of the spoils from the Medes of the battle of Marathon."

inhabitants of the Marathon area began to worship the battle's dead as heroes, as the relative inscriptions have revealed (Inscriptiones Graecae II, 471, 26, 69). Around 460 B.C., the Athenians erected a simple trophy of white marble that consisted of an Ionic column 10 meters high surmounted by a statue of Nike. Plato made some relevant statements about this in Menexenus: "the Marathon warriors were the first to erect the trophies of their victories with the barbarians and the first to teach the other Greeks that Persian might was not invincible and that, no matter how great the wealth or how numerous the crowd of people, both can be subjugated by virtuous bravery" (Menexenus, 240d). The success of the battle has also been portrayed in many works of art. In the Poikile Stoa, there was a large painting depicting the battle that was the work of the painters Micon and Panaenus, the brother of Pheidias.

The Athenians continued to propagandize their contribution to the national struggle against the Persians as proof of the purity of their intentions. When in the middle of the fifth century B.C., Athens launched its ambitious plan for a Panhellenic policy in which it wanted be the dominant center in Greece, the Marathon victory was the main reference point and tool, and it was used to make promises of future political actions. This picture of the Athenian contribution to national Greek problems was so strong in the national subconscious mind and also in the minds of politicians that it had its final beneficiary effect following the Athenian defeat in the Peloponnesian War (404 B.C.). The Corinthian proposals to destroy Athens and sell the population into slavery was rejected by the Lacedaemonians on the grounds that this city had offered great services in the struggles of the Greeks against the barbarians, first at Marathon and then at Salamis and Plataea. This fact alone reveals the effect of the Marathon victory on the Greek people, and the clear existence of a uniform national identity. The great success resounded through the ages, and was later accepted by the Romans who were always open to influences by the ancient Greek civilization. The biographer Cornelius Nepos comments: "Nothing till the present time has become more glorious than that battle, as never before had such a small force defeated so great a number forces" (Miltiades).

On the military tactic level, the victory at Marathon proved the superiority of the Greek phalanx over the Persian archers and light infantry. At the ideological level, it showed the superiority of Greek culture over the multicultural mix that the Persian Empire was at the time. The homogeny of the Greek army, in itself a reflection of the organic unity, and, not only of the institution of the city state but also of the autonomy of the Greek nation, stood against the multifaceted nature of the Eastern world and against their mixed politics and indefinable ancestral blood lineage. The Persians conscripted numerous races, not only for their army's requirements for men and logistics, but also in order to justify their declarations and ambitions for the creation of an international empire under the Great King. Therefore, the Greek victory at Marathon was not merely a repulse of Persian military might, but it also maintained the Greek way of life itself and all the features that characterize the Greek nation.

An inscribed stele of the 490-480 B.C. period that defines how the archons of the Heracleian competition were elected. The competition was established after the battle.

The battle of Marathon
The legendary dimension of the battle

When the runner returned from Sparta where he had gone to seek help, he told the Athenians that, as he was crossing Arcadia, he had met the god Pan. Pan had complained that the Athenians had been neglecting to worship him and "ordered him to ask the Athenians why they did not worship him anymore" (Herodotus 6, 105). He also assured him of having done his best for the city as "he wished the best for the Athenians and he had, in many cases till now, been useful to them and would also prove useful in the future" (Herodotus 6, 105). What he said was true; as the god had created panic among the Persians with his wild cries, as the Marathon warriors had testified. (The word "panic" derives from Pan). As a token of their gratitude to Pan, the Athenians built a sanctuary inside a cave on the northwestern slope of the Acropolis hill. In this cave there was a statue of Pan with the following inscription by Simonides of Ceos: "I, the goat-footed Pan from Arcadia, who is against the Medes and for the Athenians, have been erected here by Miltiades." It seems that, behind this legend, lurks a belated importation into Athens of the worship of a god that was strictly Arcadian and protected pastoral life.

The site of the battle itself was so much identified with mythological tradition that it was justly seen as the place of origin of the Greek race. Marathon derived its name from a local hero, Marathus, or from a hero

The great victory of the Athenians and Plataeans over the "golden-clad Medes" at Marathon did not have a contemporary historian who could precisely describe the actual events. As is natural, when Herodotus undertook to do so, many events had been forgotten while others had been changed. The main thing is that the battle was soon surrounded by the aura of a very charming myth that can, perhaps, be allowed to wander forever over the battlefield.

of the same name in Arcadia. King Cecrops was the first to collect the population of Athens in that area and retain it in one city, Dodecapolis. Xouthos, the son of Hellene and grandson of Deucalion, who had been exiled from Thessaly because of his brothers, took refuge in Attica. Once there he wedded Kreousa, the daughter of King Erechtheus, and founded Tetrapolis by uniting four separate townships – Marathon, Oenoe, Tricorinthos, and Provalinthos. His sons, Ion and Achaeus, are considered to be the ancestors of the Ionians and Achaeans. It was also on the Marathon plain that the battle between the Heracleids and the Athenians against the Argives was fought. And Theseus is also said to have done one of his brave deeds there: the capture of the fierce Marathonian bull named Taurus.

It was thus natural that on this sacred site of Marathon, the gods

The dog of Marathon

The Roman writer Aelianus (second-third century A.D.) wrote that a large dog participated in the battle of Marathon, at the side of his master hoplite, and that the dog attacked, with vicious bites, each Persian soldier who fought against his master. Aelianus further adds that the dog had been depicted in the Panaenus' painting of the battle of Marathon and Micon that was in the Poikile Stoa. It is possible that there were more dogs than just this one and that they were used for guarding the camp, on patrols, and even to attack the Persians in aid of the phalanx. If this assumption is correct, the painters may have used the depiction of a dog in order to honor these faithful battle companions of the Athenians.

Ten years later, Xerxes brought hundreds of war dogs to use during his campaign against Greece. Something similar was done by Alexander during his Asian expedition and also by King Pyrrus, who used the famous dogs of Hepirus in many battles.

would hasten to the support and aid of the Athenian and Plataean hoplites. Theseus suddenly appears, emerging from the ground, ready to help his descendants. "Many thought that they had seen the apparition of Theseus, walking in front of them against the barbarians" (Plutarch, Theseus). The demigod Heracles also suddenly appeared, holding his terrible club, and hastened to fight on the side of the saviors of his children, while the goat-footed Pan, accompanied by his Panisks, came and dispersed the Persian phalanxes. The goddess Athena could not, of course, be left out of the concert of all these gods and she appeared on the battlefield, or rather in the eyes of the Marathon warriors, fully armed, leading a four-horse war chariot, and consumed by vindictive wrath against those who dared to threaten the city she protected. On Athena's side, many Marathon warriors also thought they saw Artemis with her murderous arrows and the frightening goddess Hecate.

During this battle, it was not just heroes, gods, and demigods that participated, but also certain unfamiliar and strange entities that have since given birth to many theories that stretch the limits of one's imagination. According to Pausanias (Attica, 32, 5), at the height of the battle, a man suddenly appeared in the clothes of a peasant, holding a long weapon resembling a plough. The man in question was observed killing many Persians and disappeared as suddenly as he had come when the battle ended. "When the Athenians asked about him, the god said nothing except that they had to honor the hero Echetlaeus (εχέτλη=the handle of a

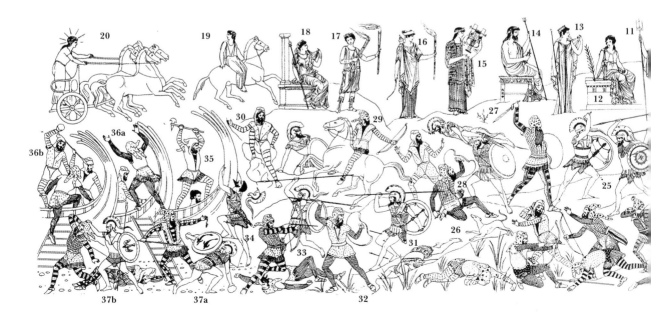

plough)" (Pausanias, Attica, 32, 5).

Herodotus mentions one more mysterious event: "And it happened also that a miracle occurred there of this kind: an Athenian, Epizelos the son of Cuphagoras, while fighting in close combat and proving himself a brave man, was deprived of the sight of his eyes, having received neither a blow in any part of his body nor having been hit with a spear or arrow, and for the rest of his life from this moment he continued to be blind, and I was informed that he used to tell about what had happened to him a tale of this kind, namely that it seemed to him that a tall man in full armor stood against him, whose beard covered his whole shield; and this apparition passed him by, but killed his comrade who stood next to him" (Herodotus, 6, 117).

All of the above stories may be the result of the distorted imagination of various warriors under the stress of the intense battle and the exhaustion of the moment. As the hoplites fought, weighed down with armor and weapons and in the high summer temperatures, for a long period of time, it is certain that some warriors

A depiction of the Battle of Marathon that was made by joining broken pottery shards and which decorated the Poikile Stoa of the Agora of Athens. According to ancient sources, the painting was the work of Micon and Panaenus. The primary reference source for the painting is Pausanias (Attica, 15, 3). The upper part of the picture show the gods and heroes who are either watching the battle or helping the Athenians: Selene (1) on her horse, the local hero Marathon (2), the demigod Heracles (3) with his club in his right hand, his lion's head cover in his left and holding a bow, Theseus (4) emerging from the Earth's depths to participate in the battle, the mysterious Echetlaeus (5) attacking with his plough, the goddess Athena (6) fully armed on her four-horse chariot galloping to battle, the goat-footed Pan (7) ready to spread panic among the invaders, the goddess Peitho (8) looking thoughtful, Aphrodite (9) with Eros (10) watching the battle, Poseidon (11) holding his trident, Hellas (12) appearing as a seated woman holding an olive tree branch in her right hand, Hera (13) crowned and holding a scepter, Zeus (14) seated and holding his scepter, Apollo (15) with his lyre, Artemis (16) holding a bow in her right hand and a torch in her left, ready to assist the Athenians, Apate (17) holding two torches and, perhaps, implying Miltiades' tactics, Asia (18) seated on an ornamental throne and holding her scepter, Eos (19), the Sunrise goddess, galloping, Helios (20), the sun god, on his chariot. The images of Helios (Sun) and Eos (Dawn), first from right to left, and of Selene, last from right to left, lead us to the conclusion that the painting should be read starting at Helios, the Sun rising at dawn, and ending at Selene, the Moon, at nightfall. However, the next two rows of images showing the battle must be read from right, where there is the charge of the Athenians and Plataeans, to left, where there is the fighting around the ships. On the painting's right side, the Plataeans (21a) are depicted running to assist the Athenians (21b). The depiction of Miltiades (22) stands out. The Persians (23a, 23b, 23c) are trying to resist. Artaphernes (24) fights heroically. Epizelos (25) is attacking his opponents with great force. The depiction of a dog (26) and his master (27) taking down a Persian soldier (28) is impressive. Many Persians (29) are retreating and pushing one another (30) and falling into the nearby swamp. Callimachus (31) and Datis (32) are dueling. Aeschylus (33) is fighting heroically, while his brother Cynaigeiros (34) is holding a Persian ship and trying to stop it from sailing, while a Persian (35) is raising his ax, ready to deal the deadly blow to the Athenian hero. The Persians (36a, 36b) are trying to board their ships, pursued by the Athenians (37a, 37b).

suffered from heat stroke and began to experience hallucinations. In addition to these considerations, it must not be underestimated the strong religious sentiment of the Greeks. It may have caused, by way of projection, the impression that the gods were among their ranks and fighting alongside them, thus giving them additional psychological stamina and contributing to their victory.

Heracules, under the supervision of goddess Athena, defeats the lion of Nemea. According to the Marathon fighters, the demigod Heracles stood by their side in support of their struggle against the Persians.

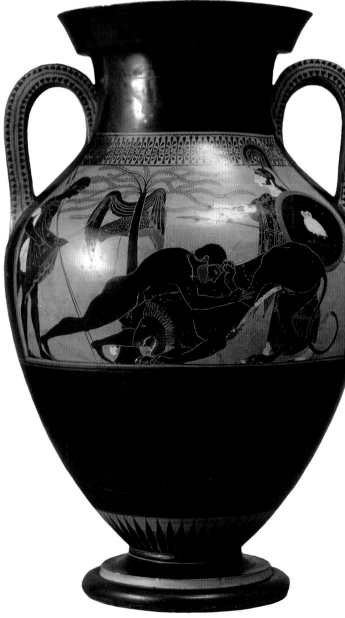

The appearance of gods is a common experience among Greeks. Athena had once guided Odysseus and all the Olympian gods had appeared many times on the battlefields of the Trojan War. In a miraculous sequel, the defenders of Constantinople had seen the Holy Virgin on its "god-protected walls," aiding them. Theodoros Kolokotronis, the Greek general of the 1821 Revolution, saw that God had signed for the independence of Greece, while the Greek soldiers of 1940 had in Greko-Italian war often seen visions of Christ's Holy Mother leading them to victory. "He saw the figure of a woman, tall and slender, lightly stepping, with her head cover falling over her shoulders. He recognized her, he had always known her, and he had heard her songs being sung to him when he was a dreaming baby in the cradle. She was the great mother, magnanimous in pain and in joy, the wounded lady of Tinos Island, the General who protected those in battle" (Agelos Terzakis: The Greek Epic Struggle of 1940-1941). The truth is that Greek warriors, whatever name they used to call their gods and deities across the passage of time, have always sought their help for victory and recognized it when it came.

Pausanias states that in his own time, about 700 years after the battle, one could hear the clanging of arms, the whinnying of horses, and the shouts of men on the battlefield of Marathon. Some might say he exaggerates. But, even today, it is a certainty that others will stand up and say that, on a recent walk in Marathon they thought they could hear the sounds of battle.

The announcement of victory
Reality or legend?

The story of Pheidippides is so universal - since the establishment of the Greek state, numerous generations of Greek children have grown up with it - that it cannot be questioned, although it would be easy to doubt its validity.

The Athenian messenger covered 440 kilometers, under the summer sun, within four days, and it is likely that he had just one day, or even less, to rest before obtaining the Spartans' answer to the call for help. After returning to Athens, he continued on to Marathon, covering the additional 42 or 34 kilometers, depending on which road he followed. On the next day, or the day after that, he fought alongside his fellow citizens for two or three hours under the summer, albeit early morning, heat wearing his armor weighing about 32 kilograms. When the fighting was over, and even though he was wounded, he ran to tell his fellow citizens the news, covering an additional 42 (or 34) kilometers, possibly bleeding, but still wearing armor. Pheidippides' performance seems to be beyond the limits of the possible. Today, it is considered impossible for a decathlon champion or long-distance runner to attain such high-performance figures, even with the aid of performance-enhancing drugs. Even after taking everything into account, we find it hard to accept that the ancient Greeks, who were much more athletic and in better physical condition than the Greeks of today, could achieve such high performances. Furthermore, why did

When the Athenians heard of the Persian landings at Marathon, they sent the runner Pheidippides to ask the Lacedaemonians for help. Pheidippides covered the distance from Athens to Sparta in two days (1,140 furlongs or 220 kilometers). After receiving the ephors' reply, he began his return to Athens immediately. Following the delivery of the message, he went to Marathon and took part in the fighting. Once the battle had ended, he collected his weapons and, still wearing his armor, wounded as he was, he ran to tell the momentous news to his anxiously waiting fellow citizens. On arrival, the only word he was able to utter before falling dead from exhaustion was «Νενικήκαμεν» ("We obtained the victory").

they choose the exhausted, wounded Pheidippides to carry out the mission for a second time when they could have chosen another, well-rested, fresh runner?

If Herodotus is taken as our primary source of information, then it is seen that he mentions the sending of Pheidippides to Sparta but makes not the slightest mention of the announcement of the victory to the Athenians of the city after the end of the battle. Plutarch, drawing his information from the nonextant work of Heracleides of Pontos, mentions the incident, but his words are not very clear: "As Heracleides of Pontos states,

An artist's impression from the 19th century, depicting the death of the Marathon runner after announcing the victory.

Thersippos of Erchia announced the battle of Marathon. But most say that it was Eukles who, running with his armor on, perspiring from the battle and falling at the doors of the nobles, could only say 'Rejoice! We are rejoicing!' («χαίρετε, χαίρομεν»), and immediately expired" (Plutarch, 347C).

Lucian states, "Philippides, the first man who ran from Marathon to announce the victory, said, "Rejoice, we are winning!" («χαίρετε, νικῶμεν») to the presidents who were in a meeting and were worried about the outcome of the battle, and then expired after saying this, uttering with his last breath the word "Rejoice" (Lucian: The Dialogues of the Gods). The first problem arises from the name. Was it Philippides, as Lucian

states, or Pheidippides? Are these two men the same person or two different individuals? The similarity of the two names leads us to think that Lucian, the historian from Samosata, used a name that had been corrupted with the passage of time. The second problem is more obvious: Who delivered the message, Philippides or Thersippos? It is impossible to discover the answer to this question. Many could claim that the messenger was Thersippos, since Pheidippides would have been too exhausted after his journey from Sparta to Athens. However, others might equally claim that if Pheidippides had been selected to go to Sparta, he must have been the best and fastest runner and, therefore, it would have been he who would have been chosen again to bring the news of victory from Marathon. Professor Evangelos Albanides of the Democritean University of Thrace, who has researched this matter in detail, poses one more question: "Why is there no reference to the matter at all in Herodotus' History? It is a known fact that Herodotus enriched his "History" texts with a multitude of informational items. Because of his insatiable curiosity to see and know everything, he was often driven to the point of interrupting his historical narrative, launching into various other subjects with geographical and ethnological dimensions, and into forays of purely literary creativity. How is it then possible that he did not touch on the matter of the Marathon runner?" (Evangelos Albanides, The Messenger of the Marathon Victory).

What can be initially assumed is that the particular incident is a legend that was "added" after the battle, to give it a more heroic dimension. However, it does not seem possible that the victory was not announced in Athens. According to Philostratos' testimony, there were specially trained long-distance runners who were tasked with bringing news concerning military battles and their results. In 668 B.C., for example, the people of Ilia were waging war against the Dymaians. The decisive battle took place on the final day of the Olympic competitions. The Ilians defeated the enemy, and a messenger ran to announce the news of victory to those in the stadium at Olympia, arriving just as the awards were being presented. Another incident, very

A view of the tomb of the Athenians who fell in the Battle of Marathon. (Photo by Nikos Giannopoulos, June 2007)

similar to the one at Marathon, occurred after the Battle of Plataea. According to Plutarch, a runner by the name of Euchidas ran the distance from Plataea to Delphi and back to Plataea (about 1,000 furlongs, i.e., 185 kilometers) and fetched the sacred flame from the Delphic Oracle, falling dead on his return to Plataea.

There are many other such examples leading to the conclusion that an announcement of victory was a common occurrence in antiquity. It is possible then that Herodotus considered it not worthy of mentioning, especially as the 42-kilometer distance that separated Athens from Marathon was negligible when compared to the 440 kilometers already run by Pheidippides.

There are two further questions that must be dealt with. First, why did the Athenians send a runner to announce the victory when they could easily have used sun signals that were commonplace at that time, as the sun signal of the unknown conspirators to the Persians has shown. While this first question cannot be answered, the second relates to the security of the message itself. A mounted messenger would have taken a road that was mainly semicoastal (Rafina-Pikermi-Pallene-Stavros Agias Paraskevis-Chalandri-Athens), where he would have run the risk of falling into an ambush, as no one really knew where the Persian cavalry was at that time. So, a runner had been preferred who would follow the semimountainous yet safer route (Vrana-Ekali-Kiffissia-Psychiko-Athens).

The story of the messenger, whether true or not, made a great impression on the French academician and devout Philhellene, Michel Bréal. It made him propose and establish the first ever long-distance run from Marathon to Athens at the first modern Olympic Games of 1896.

The starting point for the athletes of the Marathon race at the Municipal Stadium of Marathon. It is from here that the athletes started their Marathon run in the Olympic Games of 2004. (Photo by Nikos Giannopoulos, June 2007)

The Greeks and Persians at Marathon
The protagonists' fighting spirit

The victory of the Athenians and Plataeans at Marathon resembles all military victories in that it cannot only be interpreted through examination of military tactics, weapons, or sheer bravery. Each army and each common soldier has a particular historical background, comes from a particular social environment, and is characterized by beliefs and moral values that dictate the way the army and its soldiers fight and why they fight. The Athenians themselves, as well as contemporary Westerners, saw the Greek victory as an expression of a cultural and ethnic superiority of Greece (and the West) over the "barbarian" of the Near East, giving us in this way an appreciation that was more composite in nature and more interesting than previous ones. What was the cultural and social foundation of the protagonists? What were their weaknesses and their strong points? Was the Athenians' victory "inevitable" and "natural" or was it the result of a combination of various other factors?

The Greeks: Citizen soldiers

The Greek world was a world of "cities," i.e., it was a world of communities of free men with their homes, united by a tradition of common religious worship and common ancestral myths. Plataea, as opposed to Athens, can be taken as a better example of a typical city-state, as the latter encompassed a huge territory when compared to other Greek cities of the time. The small scale of these communities allowed closer interpersonal relationships among their inhabitants

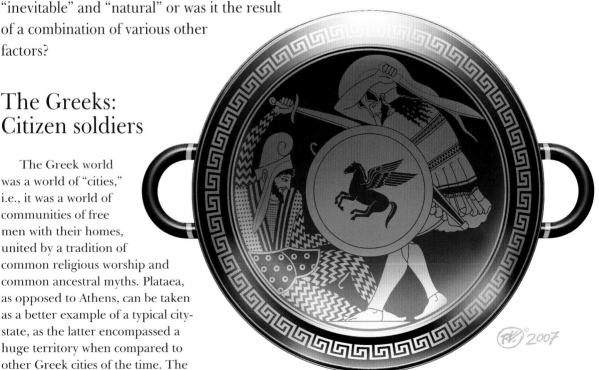

An Athenian hoplite strikes down his Persian opponent. An illustration based on a red-figure cylix cup from Attica, from Edinburgh Museum. (illustration by Romilos Fronimidis)

A feline god from the palace of Darius I at Susa.

and was the foundation of their political and military organization - a organization that placed the utmost importance on collective and individual freedom and on equal participation in social life. The fact that each citizen possessed his own land on which his family lived provided, in tangible, material terms, a feeling of self-sufficiency and individual freedom and pride. But, this had not always been the case. Until 510 B.C., one ruler, the tyrant, who used both violence and good relations with the Athenian aristocracy as his ruling tools, had governed Athens, like many other cities. After 508 B.C., public offices became electable, while the Public Assembly became the body that made all the decisions. At the same time, each municipality (each "deme") began to send at least one local representative to the city's council, which convened almost every day within the city and decided on current affairs in conjunction with the elected leaders (the "archons"). This renewed spirit of participation in public affairs determined the manner in which the

citizens viewed the question of war: It was now a collective, communal matter, both in terms of decisions to be made and how the war was to be fought. The men who would risk their lives in battle were also the ones who decided if it was worth a fight. And such factors came into play more often than we think. Two neighboring cities could easily come into conflict with each other on a border dispute or for matters related to their prestige. After 520 B.C., Athens, in particular, had acquired sufficient self-confidence to develop ambitions of becoming a greater power and gaining leadership in the region. Because of such ambitions, Athens decided to assist its weak Plataean neighbors in their conflict against Thebes, a city with the ambition of dominating all Boetia, and it also decided to help the Ionians in their uprising against the Persians in 499 B.C.

It is true that such a dynamic society the citizens were not one unified and undifferentiated body insofar as their views were concerned. It is characteristic that among the Athenians there existed a pro-Persian faction that went so far as notifying the Persian fleet, after the Marathon battle was over, that Athens stood defenseless. The former tyrant, Hippias, had escorted the Persians on their Marathon campaign in the hope of regaining his former power in the city. After the danger was repulsed, leading Athenians were accused of being traitors and exiled, although the accusation of being Pro-Persian was, at that time, an easy way and a tool to deal a blow to one's political opponents. As a result, the decision to make war against the Persians was far from unanimous, and the minority was not necessarily obliged to respect the view of the majority. Freedom was such a significant part of social life that such a strong, broad conception of it could easily lead to its negation.

Such a mentality did not favor a clear military hierarchy and discipline in the sense we use and act on today or in the sense the Persians possibly had of it at the time. It is true that the Athenians had their 10 generals, one from each tribe, elected to serve for a year under the formal command of a polemarch, who had himself also been elected. It is indicative that, in order to reach the decision to fight at Marathon, they all had to vote and it was not merely a case of issuing one more order. Even in their relations with the citizens, the generals relied more on their personal influence and example rather than on their authority and the use of violence. Their position dictated that they fight in the front line, and it is, therefore, no surprise that the polemarch Callimachus and the general Stesilaus were among the 192 dead from the Marathon battle. This military command system was, no doubt, cumbersome, but it was suitable for maintaining a high fighting spirit that was more important above all else for the Greeks. In addition, the way the Greeks fought was based on man-to-man combat, was basically simple, and did not include complicated plans and maneuvers. We cannot even be certain if the famous "encirclement" of the Persians at Marathon occurred because of a plan or through pure chance. Victory always depended on the personal bravery of each citizen and his interaction with his fellow citizens without depending on the "enlightened" guiding hand of a leader. The victory offering to the Delphic Oracle features the name of the Athenians inscribed on it as a group and not the name of their general, Miltiades. Every adult citizen who could afford the expense fitted

himself with a round, wooden shield, a bronze helmet, and a spear. The breast armor cuirass (metal, linen, or leather), the metal leg greaves, and the sword were the secondary, additional weapons that depended on the purchasing power of each citizen. These citizen warriors, the "hoplites," would stand in a battle line, one next to another in ranks, and would fight man-to-man as one body, using the shield and the spear. Those who could not afford to buy the elementary weapons (shield and spear) would fight by throwing stones and javelins while being protected by the hoplites in front of them. It is uncertain if such lightly armed men took part in the Marathon battle, as they would never have been able to confront the Persian archers on equal terms. The latter, with their greater strike range and the advantage of the high precision of their bows, could easily have keep lightly armed warriors at a safe distance. Furthermore, the Athenians and Plataeans did not, at this time, have any cavalry force worthy of the name. Horses were only used by a few rich citizens as transport to the battlefield, and they were not used during the fighting. In comparison with the Persian army, the armies of Platea and Athens consisted of fewer different elements and, therefore, lacked the ability to adapt to different roles.

The Athenians and Plataeans who faced the Persians at Marathon in 490 B.C. were not professionals and had received no military training. It is doubtful whether the "adolescence" - the term used for the military service of the Athenians in the fourth century B.C. - existed at the beginning of the fifth century B.C. in the form in which it later developed. The Athenians themselves had, for many years, been expounding the importance of natural-born virtue for victory and not of the military training acquired later in life. Exercising the body by wrestling was a basic component in the education of the elite, but it did not feature any military exercises apart from the possible exception of the "hoplite race" in which the racers wore a helmet and carried a shield. Following the overthrow of Hippias and the establishment of democracy, there developed an increased awareness of responsibility toward the fellow citizens of one's city that led, in turn, to an increase in fighting morale. This morale was further strengthened and revitalized by the Athenians' participation in battles against the Spartans (509 B.C.-508 B.C.), the Boetians and the Chalcideans (506 B.C.), and against the Aeginetans (in the 490's decade B.C.) and the Persians (499 B.C. - 498 B.C.). Experience and a sense of invincibility had by now boosted their self-confidence. The strength of the Athenian hoplites now lay in their enthusiasm and morale and not in their military training and skills. This, of course, is not to say that the Athenians were fearless. The mere view of the Persians at Marathon caused great awe, and Miltiades was hard put to convince his fellow citizens to fight against the Persians, with his efforts only succeeding after the highly feared Persian cavalry had departed.

Why did the Athenians remain alone to fight against the Persians? To begin with, the conception of Greek identity, however that was conceived at the time, was a secondary consideration for the ancient Greeks when it competed with the local identity and the freedom and fame of their city. As a result, most Greek cities viewed the danger of being dominated by a distant power in the East as less of an evil and less frightening than the danger of being dominated by a hated neighbor and competitor. It was this that was the main reason that the majority of cities gave the Persian delegates "earth and water" as tokens of submission before 490 B.C. The proud Spartans and Athenians had refused to do so, but the former had delayed to send their reinforcements to Attica. When the 2,000 Lacedaemonians finally reached Marathon, the battle had already ended. The only people who aided the Athenians were the Plataeans, who had been supported earlier by the Athenians in their fight against their powerful and hated neighbors from the city of Thebes and, naturally, were worried that if they lost their strong protector they would eventually not be able to ward off the Thebans unaided. In addition, Plataea was the only city in close proximity with which the Athenians had good relations. The other nearby cities of Chalkis, Thebes, Megara, and Aegina were cities against which Athens had recently fought, and so wished to see their destruction. If examined in the light of political common sense, the decision by Athens to stand against the Persians was almost suicidal, but was also compatible with its cultural background. However, in order to fully comprehend why the Athenians emerged victorious, the background of the Persian warriors must also be placed under close scrutiny.

The bronze head of a vulture from a pot of Asiatic origin. (Archeological Museum of Olympia)

The Persians: The king-polemarch and his warriors

The Great King was, above all, a polemarch. He led his men to war in order to stifle uprisings, like those of the Egyptians and Babylonians, to repulse invaders such as the northern nomadic tribes, and to expand his territory. Through war, the leader gained more prestige, consolidated his authority, and increased his wealth. In other words, war was a "natural" activity for the Achaemenid dynasty kings. But, they did not always conduct their wars in person. For the 490 B.C. campaign, Darius had sent his nephew Artaphernes as his representative, while actual command of the army was in the hands of Datis, an experienced general of the Medes.

The aristocracy from the Iranian highlands was also given the most important of the empire's military commands. It was bonded to the king by strong interpersonal relationships that were regularly strengthened through marriage, celebrative feasts at the royal court, hunting expeditions in the royal "paradise" grounds, exchanges of valuable gifts, and awards of high positions to favored henchmen, the so-called "bandaka." Within this elite, the Persian noblemen were the most favored class. The moral set of beliefs and codes of this elite class was the main system of values that strongly influenced and shaped the fighting spirit and the army's tactics. As Herodotus describes in a few brief words, "the Persian nobles learned three things from a young age: to ride horses, to use the bow, and to tell the truth." However, this was not an established training process as it was in the Spartan or Roman army. It was, rather, a way of educating the new noblemen within the royal court with the aim of forming a faithful warrior cadre and loyal subjects of the King. Indeed, it was similar in many ways to the processes seen in many military aristocracies – e.g., those of Medieval Europe or of the Japanese samurai. The moral integrity of these men was certainly not inferior to that of their Greek counterparts. It is even possible that Datis was killed while fighting among his men at Marathon.

The existence of interpersonal relations between the king and the noble polemarchs was not only a guarantee of obedience, but it also influenced the relationship between the king and his troops. In his public inscriptions, the Persian king made frequent and special mention of his personal ties to his soldiers and of the need for them to be faithful to their king. There was always a danger that ambitious provincial military commanders would use their regional armies against his central power to either gain independence or to usurp his throne. The promises of devotion to the king were rewarded by the bestowal of material goods (e.g., lands or other gifts) that were proportional to the services rendered to the king. This emphasis on blind devotion to the king and on close interpersonal relationships between the king and his warriors reminds one of the feudal practices of medieval Europe. However, it was foreign to the ancient Greeks, who saw it as a form of slavery and as alien to their own system of values. The Greeks would later repeatedly state that their military superiority was derived from the fact that they fought out of respect for the law, not out of fear of the commanders' whip who stood behind them and pushed them forward. Without doubt, such an interpretation of the fighting spirit of the Persians is too simplistic and does not take into full consideration the role played by the weight of the personal relationship with the king. If, for the Greeks, the major motivation for fighting was devotion to impersonal law – an entity that was over and above any actual personal relationships – then, for the Persians, such motivation was devotion to the law as personified by the King. Before we hasten to term this attitude as "oriental" mentality, let us remind ourselves that a similar ideological conception of absolute monarchy thrived in "enlightened" Europe (and later also in Greece) until the 19th century.

The nucleus of Darius' army consisted of the 10,000 Immortals who were Medes and Persians. Among them were the 1,000 elite Persian warriors who were the King's personal guard. In addition to this infantry force, the King's regular forces also included 1,000 horsemen who were based around the capitals of the time, Persepolis or Susa. Additional to these forces that were under the king's immediate command, each provincial ruler (or satrap) had his own forces – infantry and cavalry of mainly Iranian descent – to aid him in repulsing enemy attacks and to support the King in his campaigns whenever the need arose. Given the fact that the 490 B.C. campaign was not under the king's immediate command, the expeditionary force did not include the Immortals, but only included units from the provinces – probably from the western ones.

Persian soldiers lived in "colonies," usually in ethnic groups, and were dispersed throughout the whole of the empire. Both the Immortals and the provincial soldiers formed an elite body of warriors who received land, weapons, clothing, and food from the king as a reward for their services. They were often inspected by the king so he could check their battle-worthiness and their military readiness. The military profession, with its attendant obligations and benefits, was usually hereditary and in that sense it reminds us of the Roman army of the later Roman Empire era. The composition of the Persian army at Marathon is not absolutely known. In the center of the battle formation were the elite Persians and Scythians, but we do not know who manned the wings or rode in the cavalry ranks. It is possible they were soldiers from various ethnic groups. As the Persian army had set out from Cilicia and had stopped in Ionia, it is also possible all the units had come from Asia Minor and, perhaps, also northern Syria. Contrary to many modern views, the conscription of mere subjects must have been used for mainly defensive operations of a local scale. It may also have been designed to force undisciplined subjects, such as the Ionians – who must have manned many ships of the Persian fleet in 490 B.C. – into lawful subjection and obedience.

By the eighth century B.C., cavalry had already made its appearance in the Middle East, to answer the threat of mounted nomads from the north. However, the Achaemenids quickly transformed it into the most important corps in their army, even to the extent of replacing the chariots. This was easy, as the Iranian highland tribes, related as they were to the Scythian tribes and sharing similar economic and social backgrounds and structures, had a long tradition of horse riding behind them. The Persian cavalry was the spearhead of the army's attacks. Wearing a metal helmet and a scaled cuirass, carrying a javelin and short sword, and riding heavy horses, although without a saddle and stirrups, the Persian horsemen would attack their enemy, firing arrows as they advanced and then throwing their javelins as they neared their opponents. The great depth of their formations in combination with their loose battle array allowed each rank of horsemen to turn around as soon as it reached the enemy front line and retreat through the gaps of the files, which allowed the following mounted archers to attack the enemy in their turn. When the enemy formation collapsed, the cavalry charged and relentlessly pursued them. Without doubt, the sight of the massed Persian cavalry charging on their large horses while launching torrents of arrows was enough to shake the nerve of even the most steadfast of warriors and the line infantrymen in particular. The expeditionary forced that landed at Marathon included an unknown number of cavalry, which had been transported along with their horses on suitable horse-carrying vessels. The sea voyage must have imposed a number of limitations with regard to the number of horses transported. It must be remembered that the Athenians or the Spartans possessed no cavalry units at this time. The Marathon plain was eminently suitable for a cavalry action, while it also provided grazing grounds for the horses. However, as the Athenians had no force to oppose the Persian cavalry, they dared not face the enemy cavalry on the open plain, which explains why they elected to camp on the slopes of Mt. Agrieliki, a location from which they could easily control the road to Athens. When the Persians finally decided to re-embark their army, starting with the cavalry, the Athenians, understanding that their opponent had now deprived

itself of its greatest advantage, decided to attack immediately with the result that their victory was guaranteed. It is doubtful the Athenian hoplites would have been able to repulse a Persian cavalry charge if they had faced it. At the battle of Plataea in 479 B.C., the Athenians had succeeded in repulsing the Persian cavalry due to two factors: the use of their archers and the death of the Persian army commander, Masistius.

The majority of the Persian army consisted of infantry wearing a leather cuirass (only some elite troops had a cuirass of metal scales), carried a short sword, an ax (the "sagaris"), and had a bow and short spear. The men of the first rank also had a large shield (the "gerron") made of woven bamboo reeds, or branches and leather that allowed them to form a protective wall. Protected, thus, behind this wall, the troops of the following ranks could launch their arrows against the enemy line and weaken it. When the first indications of an enemy collapse became obvious, there followed a charge and a subsequent man-to-man battle with spears, axes, and short swords. At Marathon, however, it was not the Persians who attacked first, but the Athenians! They ran, charging ahead for the last few meters – a tactic that left the Persians insufficient time to use their bows, their primary weapon, and which brought about the man-to-man combat much sooner than usual. The Persian warriors were more lightly armed than their Greek opponents for this

A bronze lebes (deep bowl) that was given as an award to Marathon athletes in the first races that were held in honor of those fallen in the Battle of Marathon.

style of battle. Mainly, they lacked a large solid shield, as even the large "gerra" shields of their first ranks were primarily designed to protect them against enemy arrows, in similar fashion to their Assyrian counterparts. Furthermore, the professional Persian warriors were equipped and trained to fight in a series of successive challenges: line of battle, man-to-man battle, and siege. That said, the elite Persians and Sacans still managed to dominate the center, breaking up the Athenian hoplites and pursuing them onto the plain. It was the defeat of the Persian wings that forced the elite troops to retreat. Eleven years later, at Plataea, the Lacedaemonians saw for themselves that the Persians were worthy opponents as they retreated only after a hard battle in which their commander Mardonius had been killed.

The birth of a nation

The operation that Darius had begun to organize in 491 B.C. was limited in its objectives: the were the punishment of Athens and Eretria for their participation in the Ionian Revolt of 499 B.C. and the conquest of all the islands he came across until his fleet reached its destination. He had already accepted the submission of many cities that had given him the tokens of "earth and water," thus recognizing his dominance. The Persian expeditionary force had, indeed, managed to seize control of the central Aegean and to destroy Eretria, while a possible victory over the Athenians could eventually lead to the return to power of the tyrant Hippias as a subject and ally of the Great King. It is not known whether the Persians would seek a further

A Greek hoplite departs for war. The illustration is based on a red-figure amphora of the sixth century B.C. from the National Exposition of Antiquities of Berlin. (illustration by Romilos Fronimidis)

battle with Sparta, the other city that had refused to give "earth and water." Even if they did not have enough time to start such a war, the existence of an Attican bridgehead would make it easier to attempt such an undertaking the following year. Artaphernes, however, did not attempt to continue his operations following his defeat in Attica, choosing instead to return to Asia. Still, the fact that the experienced Darius had assigned command of his army to others for this operation reveals to us that he considered Greece of secondary importance in relation to other regions. Indeed, the symbolic acceptance of his superiority by most Greek cities was enough to confirm the glory of his power to the world, without the need to assimilate these cities and incorporate them within the administrational and taxation structures of his empire by means of a powerful military presence on the western side of the Aegean. His army's defeat at Marathon was merely an unfortunate development of minor significance. For the Athenians, on the other hand, a possible defeat would have been a matter of life and death, as it clashed directly with the cultural principles on which their community had been founded. Their victory raised their self-confidence to great heights. The generation of the Marathon warriors took its position among the heroes of the city's mythical past and, for a long time afterward, the Athenians would remember them quite often in order to feel reassured of their superiority over the barbarians and the other Greeks. Aeschylus, who fought at Marathon, preferred to have his tombstone inscribed with words that stated that he had participated in the Marathon battle rather than with words that stated that he had been a distinguished poet. In addition, the hoplites who had borne the brunt of

A Persian Immortal from the Palace of Susa at the time of Darius I.

the fighting, now consolidated the superiority of their fighting spirit in relation to that of their lighter-armed compatriots, cavalrymen or psiloi-oarsmen, thus leading to the emergence of a pure hoplite phalanx that only consisted of heavy infantry and to stylized hoplite battle by means of an unwritten ethical code. This pure fighting spirit was retroactively imposed on the history of the battle and, by so doing, ousted the contributions of other warriors from the contemporary and later narratives of the battle. In addition, the Athenian victory showed the other Greeks that resistance against the Persians could achieve a good result. A decade later, when the Persians returned with Xerxes, Darius' son and successor, as their commander, the Greek cities not only refused to give "earth and water" to the Persians, they also united their forces to face the threat. Hellenic self-consciousness was born.

Lesser-known details

Battle memories

● As literary tradition states, Miltiades asked Artemis Agroteras (the goddess protecting the forest and the hunt) for help before the battle. He even promised her that he would sacrifice as many goats as the fallen enemies (Claudius Aelianus, Various Histories, 2, 25). Xenophon mentions the same story and reveals that, following victory, the Athenians were unable to find 6,400 goats (the number of dead Persians) and decided instead to sacrifice 500 each year until they paid off their debt.

● The polemarch Callimachus, along with other prominent Athenians, must have been killed during the battle's final phase that was fought around the ships. The Athenians were carried away by their victory, broke up their formations and began a chaotic pursuit of the broken enemy. However, by doing this, they became easy targets for the experienced Persian archers who were trying to cover the retreat of their compatriots. Plutarch, in his "Synagogue

of Parallel Greek and Roman Histories," says that the body of the Athenian polemarch was discovered punctured by many arrows.

● Immediately following the battle, Miltiades, commander of nine tribes, hastened to Athens to prevent a possible Persian landing. Aristides, with the hoplites of the Antiochis tribe, remained at Marathon to guard the rich spoils and, faithful to his morals, did not seize the opportunity to take any of the highly valuable Persian spoils for himself.

● The classical Marathon race distance (42,195 meters) that was adopted for the first time during the first modern Olympic Games in Athens in 1896 has been placed under question, as there is a greater probability that the unknown Marathon runner brought the victory proclamation to the city by way of the road that goes through the mountain and passes through the town of Kifissia. However, the organizers of that first Olympics finally opted for the longer, albeit smoother, route.

Lesser-known details

● The absence of Persian cavalry from the battlefield of Marathon gave the Athenians and Plataeans an unexpected advantage. However, in retrospect, what would have happened if the cavalry had not retreated on the eve of the battle? It is improbable that Miltiades and the other generals had not already formulated a plan that included ways of countering the enemy cavalry. In the days between the arrival of the Athenians and the start of the battle, the Athenians must have carried out many specific exercises to train the phalanx for the type of maneuver in battle that the presence of Persian cavalry would have imposed.

● The heroic struggle of Cynaigeiros inflated the myth concerning the conditions of his death. According to myth, the Athenian warrior, having first lost his arms from the ax of the Persian warrior, tried to stop the ship with his teeth! But a second fall of the ax cut off his head.

● Just one year after his apotheosis at Marathon, Miltiades met the cruel face of Athenian democracy. In 489 B.C., he attacked the island of Paros, as it had not helped Athens sufficiently during the Persian invasion, but his attack failed. Alcmeonides Xanthippos, the father of Pericles, accused Miltiades of treason. The accused was fined the enormous sum of 50 talents. Unable to pay, Miltiades was thrown into prison where he finally died of gangrene from a wound he had received in his expedition against Paros. According to Pausanias, he was buried at Marathon, far from the city that had so soon forgotten its savior.

● According to Herodotus, King Darius, following the suppression of the Ionian Revolt, and remaining angry with the Athenians who had dared to take up arms against him, gave one of his slaves the task of constantly reminding him of the insult he had received from the disrespectful Athenians with the words "Master, remember the Athenians." There is no doubt that the Persian invasion was not in any way connected with the oversensitivity of the Persian monarch. However, this anecdotal story, which comes from secondary literature rather than from history, reveals that controlling such a huge empire was such a tiring task that the Persian king could not even remember an insignificant little city-state such as Athens!

The classical-period tomb of Vranas, possibly where the Plataeans who fell in the Battle of Marathon lie buried.

Bibliography

1. Herodotus, *The Histories.*
2. Herman Bengtson, *Griechische Geschichte*, Verlag C. H. Beck, Munich, 1994.
3. J.B. Bury & R. Meiggs, *A History of Ancient Greece.* Kardamitsas Publications, Athens, 1992 (In the Greek language).
4. N.G.L. Hammond, *A History of Greece to 322 B.C.,* Oxford University Press, Oxford, 1986.
5. *A History of the Greek Nation*, Ekdotiki Athinon Publication, Athens, 1972 (In the Greek language).
6. Panayiotis Kannelopoulos, *A History of Ancient Greece,* D. Gialelis Publications, Athens, 1982 (In the Greek language).
7. H.D.F. Kitto, *The Greeks,* Penguin Books, London, 1991.
8. Claude Mossé & Annie Schnapp-Gourbeillon, *A History of Ancient Greece,* Papadimas Publications, Athens, 2000 (In the Greek language).
9. Claude Mossé & Annie Schnapp-Gourbeillon, *Athens, The History of a Democracy,* Educational Foundation of the National Bank of Athens, Athens, 1988.
10. Georg Steinhauer, *War in Ancient Greece,* Papadimas Publications, Athens, 2000.
11. Aeschylus, *The Persians.*
12. Xenophon, *The Anabasis of Cyrus.*
13. Pausanias, *Description of Greece, Books I-IX.*
14. Plutarch, *Themistocles.*
15. Plutarch, *Aristides.*
16. Plutarch, *Ethics.*
17. Suidas, *Lexicon,* Georgiadis Publications (In the Greek language).
18. Simonides of Ceos, *The Collected Works,* Cactus Publications, Athens, 1992 (In the Greek language).
19. Strabon, *Geography,* Zaharopoulos Publications (In the Greek language).
20. Herman Bengtson, *History of Ancient Greece from its Beginnings to the Roman Empire,* Melissa Publications, Athens, 1991.
21. A.R. Burn, *Persia and the Greeks: The Defense of the West, c. 546-478 B.C.,* London, 1962.
22. P. Connoly, *Greece and Rome at war,* Greenhill Books, London, Stackpole Books, Pennsylvania.
23. N.G.L. Hammond, *The Campaign and Battle of Marathon,* JHS 88, 13-57 (esp. 32-3), 1968.
24. V.D. Hanson, *The Western Type of Warfare: The Decisive Battle in Classical Greece,* translated by Marios Blettas, Constantinos Tourikis Publications, Athens (In the Greek language).
25. *A History of the Greek Nation,* Vol. II, Ekdotiki Athinon Publication, Athens, 1981 (In the Greek language).
26. K. Koliopoulos, *The Advanced Strategy of Ancient Sparta (750-192 B.C.),* Poiotita Publications, 2001 (In the Greek language).
27. G. Korres, *Marathon,* Great Soviet Encyclopaedia, Vol. 20 (In the Greek language).
28. Spyros Marinatos, *The Marathon Excavations,* Archives of the Athens Archeological Society, 1971 (In the Greek language).
29. Spyros Marinatos, *Marathon,* Archives of the Athens Archeological Society, 1970.
30. D. Maronitis, *Herodotus: Eight Novels and Four Anecdotes,* Agra Publications, Athens (In the Greek language).
31. I.K. Merenditis, *The Political and Military Structures of the Greeks during the years before the Persian Wars,* Athens (In the Greek language).
32. K. Paparrigopoulos, *A History of the Greek Nation,* Volumes 1-2, Nikas Publications, Athens, 1930 (In the Greek language).
33. V.Ch. Petrakos, *Marathon,* an Archeological Guidebook, Athens Archeological Society, 1995 (In the Greek language).
34. I. Spyropoulos, *The Histories of Herodotus,* Govostis Publications, Athens, 1995 (In the Greek language).
35. U. Wilcken, *A History of Ancient Greece,* Papazisis Publications, Athens, 1976 (In the Greek language).
36. P. Green, *The Greco-Persian Wars,* Constantinos Tourikis Publications, Athens, 1976 (In the Greek language).
37. D. N. Garoufallis, *The Persian Wars: The Titanic Struggle that Shook the Ancient World,* Periscopio Publications, Athens, 2003 (In the Greek language).
38. Alan Lloyd, *The Battle of Marathon: The crucial battle which established Athenian Democracy,* Enalios Publications, Athens (In the Greek language).
39. P. D. Karykas, Marathon 490 B.C.: "The Eternal Glory of Greece," *The History of Greeks* magazine (bi-monthly publication of the magazine

The Education of the Greeks (In the Greek language).

40. "Greek Strategy," an article in the volume HELLAS of the Encyclopaedic Lexicon of Helios (In the Greek language).

41. *Polyaenus, Stratagems,* Georgiadis Publications, Athens, 1995 (In the Greek language).

42. Liddell Hart, *Indirect Strategy,* Greek Army Headquarters Publication, 7th Staff Bureau, Publications Department, Athens 1963 (reprinted in 2002) (In the Greek language).

43. J.C. Fuller, *Decisive Battles of the Western World,* SPA Books, London, 1993.

44. H. Delbruck, *History of the Art of War - Warefare in Antiquity,* Bison Books, University of Nebraska, 1990.

45. D.N. Garoufallis, "The Battle of Marathon: The Glory of the Hoplite Phalanx," *Military History* magazine, Issue 13, September 1997 (In the Greek language).

46. D. Gedeon, "Tactical Innovations in Ancient Greece," *Military History* magazine, Issue 65, January 2002 (In the Greek language).

47. Newspaper *Eleftherotypia,* Athens, *E-Historika* (booklet), "The Battle of Marathon of 490 B.C.," Issue 232, 15th April 2004 (In the Greek language).

48. A.R. Burns, *Persia and the Greeks, the Defense of the West, c. 546-478,* London, 1962.

49. Y.T. Cuyler, *480/479 B.C., A Persian Perspective,* Iranica Antiqua 15, 1980.

50. A. Olmstrad, *History of Persian Empire,* Odysseas Publications, Athens, 2002.

51. P.H. Blyth, *The Effectiveness of the Greek Armour against Arrows in the Persian War (490-479 B.C.),* An Interdisciplinary Inquiry, University of Reading, 1977 (Ph.D. thesis).

52. Pierre Briant, *Histoire de l'Empire perse, de Cyrus à Alexandre,* Paris (Fayard) 1996.

53. G. Cawkwell, *The Greek Wars. The Failure of Persia,* Oxford, Oxford University Press, 2005.

54. J.M. Hall, *Hellenicity. Between Ethnicity and Culture,* Chicago, The University of Chicago Press, 2002.

55. N.G.L. Hammond, "The Expedition of Datis and Artafernes," *Cambridge Ancient History IV,* Cambridge, Cambridge University Press, 1988, 491-517.

56. D. Head, *The Achaemenid Persian Army,* Stockport, Montvert Publications, 1992.

57. Peter Krentz, "Fighting by the Rules: The Invention of the Hoplite Agon," *Hesperia* 71 (2002), 23-39.

58. J.F. Lazenby, *The Defense of Greece, 490-479 B.C.* Warminster: Aris & Phillips, 1993.

59. Robin Osborne, *Greece in the Making, 1200-479 B.C.,* London and New York, Routledge, 1996.

60. Van Wees H., *Greek Warfare. Myths and Realities,* London, Duckworth, 2004.

61. Plutarch, *Theseus,* translated by M.G. Meraklis, Cactus Publications, Athens, 1991 (In the Greek language).

62. Newspaper *Eleftheros Typos,* "The Unknown Aspects of the Battle of Marathon," *Phenomena* magazine, issue 13, 28 August 2002, Athens (In the Greek language).

63. Agelos Terzakis, *The Greek Heroic Epic of 1940-1941.* (In the Greek language).

64. Lucian, *The Dialogs of the Gods,* Cactus Publications, Athens, 1994. (In the Greek language).

65. Evangelos Albanides, "The Messenger of Victory and the Marathon Race," newspaper *Eleftherotypia,* magazine *E-Historica:* "The Battle of Marathon," issue 232, April 15, 2004, Athens. (In the Greek language).

66. I. Ioannides, "The True Route of the Marathon Runner," *Gymnastics and Athletism* magazine, issue 5, 1976, pages 4-6. (In the Greek language).

67. Th. Katsonopoulos, *The Historical Background and the Evolution of the Marathon Run,* Minutes of the 1st Panhellenic Congress of Athletic History and Philosophy, Trikala, 12-14 October 2001, pages 207-220, Thessaloniki, 2002. (In the Greek language).

Introductory Note

Note: A limited glossary has been provided below that covers most of the terms that may be unfamiliar to readers. It is in alphabetical order for ease of use. Words explained in the main text have not been included here.

GLOSSARY

Aegina: Aegina is the island in the bay opposite Athens. According to Herodotus, it was a colony of Epidaurus, to which state it was originally subject. Its placement between Attica and the Peloponnesus made it a center of trade even earlier, and its earliest inhabitants came from Asia Minor. Minoan ceramics have been found in contexts of c. 2000 B.C. The discovery on the island of a number of gold ornaments belonging to the latest period of Mycenaean art suggests the inference that the Mycenaean culture held its own in Aegina for some generations after the Dorian conquest of Argos and Lacedaemon. It is probable that the island was not doricized before the ninth century B.C.

Achaeans: The Achaeans (in Greek Αχαιοί, Akhaioi) is one of the collective names used for the Greeks in Homer's Iliad (used 598 times) and Odyssey.

akinakes: The characteristic Persian sidearm was the akinakes, which was short in length but could be used for both cut and thrust. It is of Scythian origin, adopted by both the Medes and Persians from at least the seventh century until the second century B.C. The sword had a short, straight, double-edged iron blade, 34-45 centimeters (14-18 inches) in length.

Aleion Plain: The Aleion Plain is the Cilician Plain (known today as the – Cukurova or "Hole Plain," and in antiquity as Aleion Pedion) below the southern slopes of the Taurus mountain range, near the modern Turkish city of Adana.

amphora: An amphora (plural: amphorae or amphoras) is a type of ceramic vase with two handles and a long neck narrower than the body that was mainly used for wine, olive oil, and other liquids.

amrtaka: Amrtaka is believed to be the ancient Iranian name of the "Immortals."

Anopaia: The path leading through the mountains to Thermopylae through which Ephialtes led the Persians to the Greeks from the rear. Some researchers say that upon learning of an alternate pass through the mountains at Anopaia to the west, Leonidas, still in command of the Greek forces, deployed a force of 1,000 Phocian hoplites to defend that pass.

Artaphernes: A Persian satrap of Sardis, connected with Aristagoras and the Naxos expedition during the time of the Ionian revolt.

Carthaginians: The inhabitants of Carthage, the capital of Phoenicia. Carthage refers both to an ancient city in Tunisia and to the civilization that developed within the city's sphere of influence. The city of Carthage is located on the eastern side of Lake Tunis, across from the center of Tunis. Originally founded by Phoenician colonists under the leadership of Elissa, Queen Dido, Carthage became a large, wealthy city and thus a major Mediterranean power until its destruction in 146 B.C. during the Third Punic War. Although the center of Punic culture was destroyed, it continued into Roman times. Rome also re-established Carthage, with it becoming one of the three most important cities of the Empire, a position that would last until the Muslim conquest when it was destroyed a second time in A.D. 698. Today Carthage is being resettled as a suburb of Tunis.

Cilicia: In Antiquity, Cilicia (Greek: Κιλικία) was a commonly used name for the south coastal region of the Anatolian peninsula, now known as – Cukurova, and a political entity in Roman times. Cilicia extends inland from the southeastern coast of Asia Minor (modern Turkey), due north and northeast of the island of Cyprus and comprises about a third of the land area of modern Anatolia. Its inhabitants were the Cilicians.

Clazomenae: Clazomenae (Greek: Κλαζομεναί/ Klazomenai, modern-day Kiliziman near Izmir in Turkey) was an ancient Ionian Greek city and a member of the Ionian Dodecapolis (Confederation of Twelve Cities). It was one of the first cities to issue silver coinage.

crest: The plume of a helmet.

crest holder: The iron part supporting the plume of a helmet.

Crotonians: The people of Croton, a city in Lower Italy.

cuirass: Body armor that protects the torso of the wearer above the waist or hips. Originally it was a thick leather garment covering the body from neck to waist. The ancient Greeks had a formed leather cuirass, a type of anatomical breastplate that was first achieved from hot, wet-formed leather. In later years, the same form was known as the bronze cuirass. Although the bronze helmet was developed at a fairly early age, bronze was not conceived as body armor for some years later.

curved slashing sword: A short, curved sword using for cutting opponents. Synonym for kopis.

Cyme: Cyme (Aeolis), an ancient Greek colony on the coast of Aeolia.

Didyma: Didyma (Greek: Δίδυμα) was an ancient Ionian sanctuary, situated on the territory of the great classical city of Miletus, the modern Didim, Turkey. The sanctuary contained a temple and oracle of Apollo, the Didymaion or "Didymaeus Apollo." In Greek, didyma means "twin," but the Greeks who sought a "twin" at Didyma ignored the Carian origin of the name. Next to Delphi, Didyma was the most renowned oracle of the Hellenic world, first mentioned among the Greeks in the Homeric Hymn to Apollo, but preceding literacy and even the colonization of Ionia. Mythic genealogies of the origins of the Branchidae line of priests, designed to capture the origins of Didyma as a Hellenic tradition, date to the Hellenistic period.

Ennea Odoi: The ancient city, originally known as Ennea

Odoi (Nine Roads), was first established by the Thracians in a bend of the River Strymon at the foot of Mount Pangaion. Xerxes passed through on his way toward Thermopylae in 481 B.C. and, according to Herodotus, buried alive nine boys and nine girls. It was a wealthy city because of the gold and silver found on Mount Pangaion and the surrounding forests that provided wood for shipbuilding. Because of these riches, it was colonized by the Athenians under Hagnon in 437 B.C. According to the historian Thukidides, Hagnon called the city Amphipolis "because it was surrounded on two sides by the River Strymon, and he built it in such a way that it was a conspicuous sight both from the sea and from the side facing the mainland where he built a long wall across the loop of the river."

Eteocypriots: The Eteocypriots were the clans who had lived on the island of Cyprus before the advent of the Greeks. Some claim that they can be traced as far back as the Iron Age.

greaves: The protecting shields for the shins of the legs worn by ancient warriors.

Hecataeus: Hecataeus of Miletus (c. 550 B.C.– c. 476 B.C.), a Greek philosopher, was the son of a wealthy family and was named after the Greek goddess Hecate. He flourished during the time of the Persian invasion. After having traveled extensively, he settled in his native city, where he occupied a high position, and devoted his time to the composition of geographical and historical works. When Aristagoras held a council of the leading Ionians at Miletus to organize a revolt against Persian rule, Hecataeus in vain tried to dissuade his countrymen from the undertaking. In 494 B.C., when the defeated Ionians were obliged to sue for terms, he was one of the ambassadors to the Persian satrap Artaphernes, whom he persuaded to restore the constitution of the Ionic cities. Hecataeus is the first known Greek historian, and was one of the first classical writers to mention the Celtic people.

Hecate: An ancient Greek goddess who is variously described as having many forms. Hesiod considered Hecate to be a daughter, with Leto, of Perses and Asteria, two pre-Olympian Titans. As in most cultures with multigenerational deities, the preceding Titans were originally the only deities worshipped by earlier Greek cultures, while the later Olympians were the deities worshipped by later invaders who conquered Greece. Some readers of mythography find elements of cultural history reflected in myth: As Hecate was one of the only Titans who kept power and status after the Titans lost their war with the Olympians – she was always regarded as having great favor with the Olympian Zeus, and it seems likely that Hecate's cult was so strong that it could not be suppressed by the invading new religions. As with many ancient mother or earth goddesses she remained unmarried, had no regular consort, and is often said to have reproduced via parthenogenesis. Another of her attributes is that she is the mother of many monsters, including Scylla, who represented the dreaded sides of nature that elicited fear as well as awe. Hecate is also said to have had a special role at three-way crossroads, where the Greeks set poles with masks of each of her heads facing in different directions. In this form, she was known as the Goddess of the Crossroads. The crossroad aspect of Hecate stems from her original sphere as a goddess of the wilderness and untamed areas. This led to sacrifice to assure safe travel into these areas. This role is similar to lesser Hermes, that is, a god of liminal points or boundaries.

Hellenes: The Greeks by another name of Greek derivation. The word derives from "Hellas," Greece in Greek.

Hellenism: As used in the text: The Greek world of the period, including all the areas and cities where Greeks (Hellenes) lived.

helots: A class of Spartan people. The Spartans were divided into two broad categories: the residents of the pre-Doric towns, who enjoyed a free but dependent status as "Perioikoi," and the peasants, who enjoyed a far more restricted status as "helots." The "helots," or rural population, had a significantly worse status. These "helots" were tied to the land and were officially the property of the Lacedaemonian government. As a result of at least one and possibly more revolts, they were regarded with increasing suspicion and subjected to increasingly harsher laws. In fact, the Lacedaemonian government regularly declared war on the helots to enable quick retribution against any "unruly" helot without the tedious business of a trial. This unique situation led many contemporary ancient commentators to remark on the "exceptional" harshness of the Spartan system.

Heracleides of Pontos: Heracleides of Pontos (Greek: Ηρακλείδης Ποντικός) (387 B.C.-312 B.C.), also known as Heraclides Ponticus, was a Greek philosopher who lived and died at Heraclea Pontica, modern-day Karadeniz Erezli, Turkey.

hoplite: A heavily armed foot soldier in Greek armies, typically of the citizen class.

hoplon shield: Another name for the Greek shield. A hoplon shield (or simply "hoplon") was a deep-dish shield made of wood. Often, particularly later, the wood was covered in a sheet of thin bronze. During some periods, it was the convention to decorate the shield. While, during others, it was usually left unadorned. Probably the most famous shield decoration is that of the Spartans: a red capital lambda (Λ). Athenian hoplites commonly used the Little Owl, while the shields of Theban hoplites were often decorated with a sphinx.

Ilia: Ilia is a prefecture area in the northwestern part of the Peloponnese in Greece.

Ilians: The Ilians are people of the Ilia region, in the northwestern part of the Peloponnese in Greece.

Lacedaemon: The river plain surrounding Sparta itself, often used synonymously for the city or the Spartan state. The initial letter Λ (lambda), the Greek "L", was the shield blazon of the Spartan soldier.

Laconians: The inhabitants of the southeastern section of the Peloponnesus, named Laconia, of which Sparta was the chief city.

Lelantine War: The term Lelantine War is not contemporary but modern. Ancient authors normally refer to the War between the Chalkidians and Eretrians (ancient Greek: πόλεμος Χαλκιδέων και Ερετριέων polemos Chalkidéon kai Eretrion). The Lelantine War was a drawn-out military conflict between the two ancient Greek city-states of Chalkis and Eretria that took place in the early Archaic period, between circa 710 B.C. and 650 B.C. The eponymous reason for war was, according to tradition, the struggle for the fertile Lelantine Plain on the island of Euboea. Due to the economic importance of the two conflicting cities, the war spread considerably, with many other city-states joining one side or the other side, resulting in much of Greece being at war. The historian Thucydides describes the Lelantine War as the most widespread war in Greece between the mythical Trojan War and the Persian Wars of the early fifth century B.C.

Medes: A major Persian race, but the word is often used by Greek writers to denote all Persians regardless of whether they were Medes or Persians or other ethnicities under Persian rule. The Medes were an ancient Iranian people inhabiting the northwestern regions of present-day Iran, in roughly the areas of present day Kurdistan, Hamedan, Tehran, Azarbaijan, Esfahan and Zanjan. This area was known in Greek as Media or Medea (Μηδία, Old Persian Meda; adjective Median or Medic, antiquated also Medean). Under Assyrian rule, the Medes were known as Madayu. They entered this region with the first wave of Iranian tribes in the late second millennium B.C. (following the collapse of the Bronze Age). The Medic Wars are the Greco-Persian Wars by another name, often used by ancient Greek writers.

Median: Adjective from Mede: pertaining to the Medes.

Medic: Adjective, pertaining to the Medes (see word).

medimnus/medimnoi: In ancient Greece, a unit of dry capacity, of about 51.84 liters. One medimnus was subdivided into 6 "hecteis." Later, the medimnus changed value. In Cyprus, during the 17th century, it represented, 75.554 liters. During the 20th century, it is reported at 75.05 liters (around 2.13 U.S. bushels). Sometimes the word is spelt as "medimnos" with the plural form being "medimmoi."

Megabates: Megabates was a Persian general and admiral who lived between the early sixth century B.C. and the late fifth century B.C. He is known predominantly through the writings of Herodotus for his joint participation in the failed 499 B.C. siege of Naxos. He was sent by Darius the Great to accompany Aristagoras with 200 ships charged with the mission of annexing the small island in the Aegean Sea to the growing Persian Empire

Months of Athens: The Athenian calendar is the best known of all ancient Greek calendars. The Athenian months were named Hekatombion, Metageitnion, Boedromion, Pyanepsion, Maimakterion, Poseidon, Gamelion, Anthesterion, Elaphebolion, Munychion, Thargelion, and Skirophorion. The intercalary month usually came after Poseidon, and was called second Poseidon. Hekatombion, and hence the beginning of the year, fell in the summer.

Other Greek regions started their year at different times (e.g., Sparta, Macedonia in fall, Delos in winter).

Moralia: A large part of Plutarch's surviving essay work is collected under the title of the Moralia (loosely translated as Customs and Mores). It is an eclectic collection of 78 essays and transcribed speeches.

Myus: Myus (sometimes Myous or Myos) was an ancient city-state and was one of 12 major settlements formed in the Ionian Confederation and called the Ionian League.

Paeonians: Paionia or Paeonia (in Greek Παιονία) was, in ancient geography, the land of the Paeonians (ancient Greek Παίονες), the exact boundaries of which, like the early history of its inhabitants, are very obscure. During the reign of King Philip II of Macedon, Paionia covered most of what is now the former Yugoslav Republic of Macedonia, and was located immediately north of ancient Macedon, roughly corresponding to the modern Greek region of Macedonia, and south of Dardania (Europe), which roughly corresponds to modern-day Kosovo. To the east was the Odrysian kingdom of the Thracians, roughly corresponding to modern-day Bulgaria, while, in the west lay the Illyrian kingdom, roughly corresponding to modern-day Albania.

Panhellenic: Adjective: of, or relating to all Greece or all the Greeks.

Panionium: The Panionium (also Panionion) was, from around 800 B.C., an Ionian sanctuary dedicated to Poseidon Helikonios and the meeting place of the Ionian League. It was on the Mt. Mycale peninsula, about 100 kilometers south of Smyrna – modern day Izmir, in Turkey.

Panisks: The Panisks are small rural Pans, and are often found in mythology in the company of the goat-footed demi-god Pan as part of his entourage.

Peloponnesus: The large southern peninsula of mainland Greece, home to Laconia and other regions and connected to central Greece by the isthmus of Corinth. Its inhabitants are known as the Peloponnesians.

perioikoi: The periokoi or "dwellers around" were free men of Sparta, mainly farmers and merchants, who lacked the full citizenship of the Spartans. They lived in perhaps 80 or 100 towns and villages, which were called poleis (the plural of polis), in the less fertile land of the hills and coasts. They may have been part of a conquered people, but unlike the helots, they kept their freedom. Perhaps they were conquered earlier; perhaps the helot serfs were perioikoi who rebelled. The singular of perioikoi is perioikos. The perioikoi had their own laws and customs, could pursue any profession or trade they liked, and had their own local officials and dignitaries. They were restricted only with regard to foreign and military policy, being subject to the government of the entire territory or city-state Lacedaemon, which was run by Spartans. They were also required to provide troops for the Lacedaemonian army and to support Sparta in time of war. Because the Spartan citizens were themselves prohibited by their laws from engaging in any profession except that of arms, the Perioikoi were the professionals, merchants, and craftsmen of

Lacedaemon, and they were not prohibited from hoarding gold and silver. In short, they had a monopoly on all lucrative businesses and professions. They were the only people allowed to travel to other cities, which the Spartans were not, unless given permission. The name derives from (περί / peri, "around" and οἶκος / oikos, "dwelling, house").

phalanx: The phalanx (plural phalanxes or phalanges) is a massed rectangular military formation usually composed entirely of heavy infantry armed with spears, pikes, or similar weapons. The troops were disciplined to hold a line thus creating an almost impenetrable forest of points to the front. The phalanx is a hallmark of ancient Greek warfare. The word "phalanx" is derived from the Greek word "phalangos," meaning "the finger."

Philhellene: The Philhellenes were members of the movement that supported the Greek uprising of 1821 against the Turks – see "Philhellenic Movement."

Philhellenic Movement: The movement in support of the Greek uprising of 1821 against the Turks. The Philhellenes helped the Greeks in various ways in their war of independence after 1821 and until Greece was freed from the Turkish yoke.

Phreattys: A small coastal community situated in the port of Piraeus. The name is still used today.

Pnyx: Compared with the more famous surviving monuments of ancient Athens, such as the Parthenon, the Pnyx is relatively nondescript. It is a small, rocky hill surrounded by parkland, with a large flat platform of eroded stone set into its side, surrounded by steps carved on its slope. It is, nevertheless, one of the most significant sites in the city and, indeed, the world. For it was the Pnyx that was the meeting place of the world's first-ever democratic legislature, the Athenian ekklesia (assembly), and the flat stone platform is the bema (βῆμα), the "stepping stone" or speakers' platform. As such, the Pnyx is the material embodiment of the principle of is isigoria (Greek: ισηγορία), "equal speech"), i.e., the equal right of every citizen to debate matters of policy. The other two democratic principles were isonomia (Greek: ισονομία), equality under the law, and isopoliteia (Greek: ισοπολιτεία), equality of vote and equal opportunity to assume political office. The right of "isigoria" was expressed by the Pnyx assembly's presiding officer, who formally opened each debate with the open invitation "Tis agoreyein bouletai?" (Greek: «Τις αγορεύειν βούλεται?»), "Who wishes to speak?").The Pnyx was used for popular assemblies in Athens as early as 507 B.C., when Cleisthenes' reforms transferred political power to the citizenry. It was then outside the city proper, but close enough to be convenient. It looks down on the ancient Agora, the commercial and social center of the city. It was on this site that all the great political struggles of Athens of the "Golden Age" were fought. It was here that statesmen such as Pericles, Aristides and Alcibiades would have regularly spoken, with the Parthenon, Temple of Athena, the city's protective goddess, looking down on their deliberations.

Poikile Stoa: The Poikile Stoa or "Painted Porch," was erected during the fifth century B.C. and was located on the north side of the Ancient Agora of Athens. The Stoa was the location from which Zeno of Citium taught Stoicism. The philosophical school of Stoicism takes its name from the word "stoa," having first been expounded here. Most of Zeno's teachings and lectures to his followers were made from this porch. The Poikile Stoa was decorated by the fresco painter and sculptor Micon of Athens who, in collaboration with Panaenus, depicted the celebrated battle of Marathon. Both artists worked around the mid-fifth century B.C. What is striking about the Stoa Poikile is the contrast between the mythical and historical events portrayed. Depictions of Theseus' victory over the Amazonians and the Fall of Troy contrast sharply with the portrayal of the battle of Oinoe - the first important Athenian victory over Sparta - and the Battle of Marathon. The Battle of Marathon features as the most dominant and, as such, reveals the confidence and identity of the Athenians in the wake of the Persian Wars, particularly when compared to the two great mythical victories identified above.

psephisma: The Athenians of the fifth century B.C. seem to have used two words interchangeably to refer to what we call a "law," nomos (νόμος) and psephisma (ψήφισμα). In the forth century A.D. these words had two distinct meanings: a nomos was a "law," while a psephisma was a "decree."

scepter: A scepter, or sceptre, is a symbolic ornamental staff held by a ruling monarch, a prominent item of royal regalia resembling a mace.

Seven Sages: The Seven Sages of antiquity were Solon of Athens, Chilon of Sparta, Thales of Miletus, Bias of Priene, Cleobulus of Lindos, Pittacus of Mytilene, and Periander of Corinth.

slashing sword: A short sword, usually uncurved, used to cut down opponents; synonym to the Greek "kopis" for a sword of this type.

soft cap: A soft cap for the head, called "pilos" by the Greeks.

sparabara: A Persian shield bearer.

Strymon: The Strymon River flowed into the Aegean Sea between the Chalcidice Peninsula and the island of Thasos.

Suidas: Author of, perhaps, the most important Greek lexicon or encyclopedia. His work, the "Suda" (Σούδα or alternatively Suidas, Σουΐδας) is a massive 10th century Byzantine Greek historical encyclopedia of the ancient Mediterranean world. It is an encyclopedic lexicon with 30,000 entries, many drawn from ancient sources that have since been lost. The name is probably derived from the Byzantine Greek word "souda," meaning "fortress" or "stronghold," with the alternate name, Suidas, stemming from an error made by Eustathius, who mistook the title for the proper name of the author.

Susa: Greek: Σέλεύχεια, transliterated as Seleukeia or Seleukheia; Latin Seleucia ad Eulaeum) was an ancient city of the Elamite, Persian and Parthian Empires of Iran, located about 150 miles east of the Tigris River.

taka: A type of shield used by Persian warriors, usually horsemen on Median horses, which originated from the crescent-shaped Scythian "taka" shield of similar design.

takabara: A Persian taka shield bearer.

Taras: Taras was the ancient Greek name for modern-day Taranto, a coastal city in Puglia, southern Italy. It is the capital of the Province of Taranto and is an important commercial port as well as the principal Italian naval base. The Greek colonists from Sparta called the city Taras (Greek: Τάρας), after the mythical hero Taras, while the Romans, who connected the city to Rome via an extension of the Appian Way, called it Tarentum.

Thersippos of Erchia: Thersippos of Erchia is mentioned by Plutarch c. A.D. 100 in his Moralia, 347C in which he reports the legend of yet another runner, Eukles. "As Heracleides of Pontos states, Thersippos of Erchia announced the Battle of Marathon. But, the majority state that it was Eukles who, running in his armor hot from the battle and falling at the doors of the presidents, could only say "Be happy! We have won!" and immediately expired.

thesmothetai: The Thesmothetai were law officials, assistants to the archons, with the word meaning "establishers of judgments." These officials filled six positions of the nine original Archons. They acted as legal authorities and as magistrates for public cases as well as any private cases that did not fall under the jurisdiction of the three senior Archons. The Thesmothetai also decided when the jury courts would sit and assigned other officials to cases. This was an important position, as the Athenians loved their law-courts. Their legal system was very advanced for the age, and contemporary chroniclers refer to the fact that they were very well known for frequently resorting to the courts over all manner of disputes.

Xouthos: In Greek mythology, Xouthos (classical Greek: Ξοῦθος) was a son of Helen and Orseis and founder (through his sons) of the Achaean and Ionian nations. He had two sons by Creusa, Ion and Achaeus, and a daughter named Diomede. Aiclus and Cothus are sometimes also attributed as being his children. Euripides' play "Ion" provides an unusual alternative version, according to which Xouthos is the son of Aeolus and Cyane and Ion is, in fact, born to Xouthos' wife Creusa by Apollo. Xouthos and Creusa visited the Oracle at Delphi to ask the god if they could hope for a child. Xouthos will later father Dorus with Creusa, though Dorus is normally presented as Xouthos' brother. The Dorians are descended from Dorus, his son.

Nikos Th. Tselepides